Lou Manfredini's
Room Smarts

How to renovate, reconfigure, and decorate the areas in your home that matter most

Lou Manfredini's
Room Smarts

How to renovate, reconfigure, and decorate the areas in your home that matter most

Lou Manfredini
with Curtis Rist

Ballantine Books
New York

A Ballantine Book
Published by The Random House Publishing Group

Copyright © 2004 by Lou Manfredini
Illustrations copyright © 2004 by Harry Trumbore

www.ballantinebooks.com

Library of Congress Control Number: 2004090457

ISBN 0-345-46722-1

Text design by Michaelis/Carpelis Design Assoc. Inc.

Manufactured in the United States of America

First Edition: May 2004

10 9 8 7 6 5 4 3 2 1

Acknowledgments

Working on your home is hardly a private affair. Unlike so many things in our lives, the progress here—or, rather, *lack* of progress—is constantly on display to friends and especially family members. I am no exception to this rule, which is something that my friends seem to notice with particular relish. "Gee, *your* house isn't perfect?" they say, with glee. "What's the world coming to?" My wife, Mary Beth, and our four children carry on stoically amid the continual rubble, to their great credit. At times, I remind myself of the cobbler from the fables—you remember, the one who peddled shoes to the entire village while his own children went shoeless.

While the members of my family do indeed have shoes, they do want for a few other things. Bedroom doorknobs, anyone? How about that basement family room I've promised for the last two years? And what do you mean we should clear the garage out so we can actually fit the cars in there? My punch list—that contractor's nemesis that details the undone chores that accompany every project—is never longer than with my own house. I do need to thank my family, for enduring my somewhat quirky projects. (Anyone remember my sudden desire to add a front porch just in time for summer? And how it was finished just in time for winter?)

Truth be told, this is how it is when working on your home. Yet rather than chiding yourself (or allowing yourself to be chided!) for the fact that everything is not finished, the best approach is to flip things and start looking at the glass as half full rather than half empty. Focus on the progress you make, even if it's nothing more tangible than coming up with a plan and a schedule for getting it done. A house, by definition, is unfinished business; the sooner you understand and accept that, the sooner you'll revel in the challenges and accomplishments that lie ahead.

In sorting out the issues to address in this book, I'm indebted in no small measure to my friends, neighbors, and acquaintances—as well as the many thousands of people I meet each month traveling to hardware stores for personal appearances. The problems you bring to me, the questions you ask, and the uncertainties you have about your own project have helped me search for new ways to explain what the best projects are for your house.

The beautiful thing about home improvement is that you don't have to be an expert to get started. You just have to decide to start. Everything else will become clear, as your work-in-progress begins to unfold.

Lou Manfredini

Contents

Introduction

All of us, at some stage in our lives, find ourselves searching for our dream home. It's that magical place that awaits our discovery, maybe with a porch out front, or a winding driveway, and certainly an apple pie baking in the oven. No one was more desirous of this than some friends of mine named Jim and Helen.

The two met in high school, and married sometime after college. He works as an advertising copywriter, and she as an artist making beautiful fused-glass jewelry. For years, each time he received a paycheck or a year-end bonus, and each time she made another jewelry sale, they set aside money for a down payment on the house they would one day move to. While they yearned for something grand and comfortable, they bought the best house they could afford. It had a pair of enormous white oak trees in the yard, a curving stone wall out front, and plenty of charm on the outside. But the house on the inside seemed somewhat odd. It had just one bedroom, a grim living room lit by a single small window, no closets to speak of, and a kitchen and bathroom that predated the Eisenhower Administration. "It will work for now," Helen thought, and they planned on moving again within a year or two.

The funny thing, however, was that day never came. They grew to enjoy their neighbors, and loved taking walks along the nearby streets of grand homes. Bit by bit they worked on their own house. Jim updated the bathroom and the kitchen, and Helen suggested a wall of windows in the living room that brought in light, as well as a view of the oak trees in the yard. Eventually they had a child, then another, and ultimately added a family room out back along with a pair of bedrooms and a second bath upstairs to accommodate everyone. Over time, they stopped dreaming of moving someplace else and realized, like Dorothy in Kansas, that there's no place like home. "It became pretty clear to me that the house we loved the most was right beneath our feet," said Helen. "It holds every memory for us, and what we didn't love, we changed. All it took was commitment, and a plan."

This is the way a house can be. So often, we think that we have to make radical changes to end up with a home that matches our romantic notions. We think our happiness lies a few years down the road when we've finally saved enough money or built up enough equity in our current homes to be able to move. But let's face it, no matter what home we find, there are things that won't be perfect about it and that we will want to change. It could be a tiny house from a century ago that simply needs more space, or a contemporary mansion that carries a garish color scheme throughout and needs redecorating. We can either accept these things and suffer, or we can take charge of our homes and make changes that will transform how we live for the better. I'm here to argue in favor of spending the money and making the changes, beginning right now.

To me, there's no single better investment than your home. I don't mean just buying it and holding onto it. I mean spending the time, effort, and money to fix it up the way you want, and turn it into the place you have always dreamed of owning. For one thing, nothing is more malleable than a house; you can change every feature of it, as long as it's structurally sound. In my own house, for instance, I moved the location of every single bathroom to create a floor plan that works. And if your home is not structurally sound—something that is often uncovered only during a renovation—you'll be glad you found the problem and fixed it, rather than pretending that everything was just fine.

At the same time, the return on your investment is something that the average mutual fund manager would envy. Year in and year out, your home will grow in value. And the more you improve it in logical ways, the more it will be worth when it comes time to sell. This is the key point to focus on: No matter how much you love your home, you will likely sell it someday, and probably sooner than you imagined. The average length of home ownership, after all, is just seven years.

Thinking like a seller all the years you own your home has a double advantage. First, it will make your home worth more when it's time to sell. Just as important, it will make your experience of living there so much better. So often, I hear from people who are just about to put their homes on the market. "What can I do to quick fix things up?" they ask me, and they usually look surprised when I give them my answer: Nothing, except maybe a little paint and a little cleaning up. Reconfiguring the floor plan or slapping a new addition on your home a few months before you sell it makes no sense. Sure, you might be able to charge more for your house, but the project will also cost you plenty— not just in time and materials, but also in the aggravation of building it. As anyone who has endured a renovation project well knows, this can be a difficult journey. Why do it if you're not going to have the benefit of living with it?

In looking at your house, knowing what you can change and finding a place to begin can often be daunting. To me, the finished surfaces should wait until last. Instead, as we will discuss in the coming pages, I think it's essential to begin by focusing on the traffic flow within your home. Is it easy to walk from room to room, or does your home "dead end," as if you're maneuvering through some life-sized maze? Every house is different, as we well know, so there is no one-size-fits-all approach to what to do. I can, however, highlight some of the major possibilities beginning with design, then detailing how to revamp a room from floor to ceiling, and finally by running through the basics of adding an addition. We'll take a look at additional topics, as well, including how to make a house family-friendly, and not just for children but for older relatives as well. We'll also create a "wish list" of electrical devices that will help make a house so much more than just four walls with a door. Along the way, I'll explain about working with contractors and managing finances during a renovation. Both of these things can be difficult to do, which is why many people give up on home renovations before they've even started.

Embark on the road of renovation and you will discover—as Jim and Helen did—the dream lying hidden in your own home.

Lou Manfredini's
Room Smarts

How to renovate,
reconfigure, and
decorate the areas
in your home that
matter most

chapter ONE

A Plan to Live With

Want to fix up your home? Begin with the basics, in the form of an overall scheme.

My friends Shirley and Jason have the perfect house, but if you asked me to pinpoint what it is I love about it, it would be hard to describe. Is it a mansion? No. Is it furnished to look like some nineteenth-century museum? No. Does it have all the coolest gadgets and twenty-first-century styling you see in magazines? Hardly.

What it does have is class and comfort. It's the sort of place I could stop by with my wife and our four kids and spend the afternoon—without worrying about filing an insurance claim in the aftermath. Yet it's extremely beautiful, in that casual sort of way that makes you feel at home. The house is well built, which is evident to me, but its gracefulness is obvious to anyone who sets foot inside. There's a logical floor plan, beginning right at the entryway. The kids are able to run upstairs to their rooms, or downstairs to the play area. The living room is off the entryway, and connects to the kitchen in the rear. The dining room is also off the entryway, and connects to the kitchen from the other side. In addition, a short hallway leads directly to the kitchen, so you can carry groceries straight to it without tripping over the dinner guests in the dining room, or Aunt Susie holding court in the living room. A floor plan like this works beautifully because there are no "dead ends" to get stuck in. The house feels roomier and more private, because it allows people to choose their own routes to get from one place to another. Beyond this, there's a unity to how the house looks. It's a grand brick Georgian on the outside, but this alone does not guarantee grandeur on the inside. After all, I have been in more than a few of these that have a layout that has been chopped and diced into so many separate little rooms it looks as though it's been through the Cuisinart.

We often wonder where to put our money in a renovation in order to come up with a better home. I always argue in favor of beginning with the major systems such as the plumbing and electric, as well as the bathrooms and kitchen. This does leave the rest of the house when all that is finished, however. Fortunately, the work here can usually be accomplished for a fraction of the cost of these other areas. Beyond paint, an interior can sometimes be transformed just by the addition of a passageway from one room to another, or from a careful refinishing and restoration of the floors, walls, and woodwork. In other cases, the solution lies in a full-scale addition, which has the power to transform a house to an even larger degree. This is the costliest way to go, to be sure, and it also requires an understanding of the home's basic layout. Otherwise, the addition risks becoming one more room added to the chaos.

To help you change the way your home works for you, let's focus on how to design an overall renovation plan, as well as to develop an effective strategy for working with the contractors who will help bring it to reality.

Who Lives in These Rooms?

I worked on a house some years ago in a tony area of Chicago, which to me epitomized everything that's wrong with many of the homes we live in. While I was remodeling the basement into a children's playroom, I had to walk right by the living room, and couldn't help noticing it in all its pristine glory. It had beautiful white carpeting, so plush that walking on it would feel like wading through whipped cream. Amazingly, in a

house with three children under five, there was not a single footprint on the carpeting. I'm sure even the cleaning people vacuumed their way out of the place, just to preserve that showroom look. I commented on how gorgeous the room looked, and the homeowner agreed. "Yeah, but we never use it," he said. "We just look at it."

I did have to wonder, what's the point? If all you're going to do is look at a room, why not hang a painting of a beautiful room on the wall and spare yourself the effort? Why invest all that time and money in a room that you have no intention of ever using? Instead, the goal should be that the rooms in your house are yours to live in, not just to showcase and preserve for posterity or the occasional guest. If you use a formal living room regularly, wonderful. Create one that's as lavish as you want. But if not, then take a real look at how you live, and go from there. Need a larger family room? Colonize the living room. Need a place for the toys and the computers and the home office? Find a place that works for you, without trying to match your collection of rooms to some standard that you think exists.

The American home has evolved greatly over the years, in keeping with the lifestyle of the times. In the Colonial era, for instance, the rooms had great flow, with little more than a kitchen and a large gathering room where everyone huddled together against the elements. There couldn't be a simpler floor plan, yet it exactly served its purpose. As lives became more complicated, so did the typical floor plan. By the middle of the twentieth century, we added living rooms, family rooms, dens, and TV rooms, and before we knew it the house was a warren of little rooms with no real overall plan. For a while, we tried to unify them, most notably with the concept of a Great Room in the 1970s. This was intended to be one giant room that would contain the kitchen as well as the living spaces—harking back to Colonial simplicity—but it had one giant flaw: It tried to bring too many incompatible tasks under one ceiling. After all, who wants to have a conversation or watch TV with all that pot-banging and dishwashing going on? And who wants to have to clean up every dish all the time, just so the place looks presentable if anyone stops by? Clearly, the Great Room was little more than a Great Blunder.

I'd advocate a different approach today. And that is, instead of focusing on individual rooms or trying to bring everything together into one giant room, it's better to take a broader look at how the whole house functions. Obviously, certain rooms have their dedicated purposes. You cook in the kitchen, you bathe in the bathroom, and you can't do these activities anywhere else in the house. But as far as the rest of the rooms in your house, anything can go. Take the bedrooms, for instance. Sure, we sleep in them. But they also become the children's play and study areas, and a place for parents to climb into bed and read stories. Or take the master bedroom. We sleep here, of course, but who doesn't treasure a few stolen hours on a Sunday afternoon, to stretch out with the newspaper or maybe tune into a movie or a ballgame? Perhaps you have a home office in your bedroom, as well, where you come home

after a busy day of work and spend a couple of hours getting a head start on the next day.

The point is, rooms have taken on a multifunctional purpose that they never have before. In this, they reflect our own lives. After all, we're expected to be everything—from parents, and workers, and friends, to the occasional romantic date for our spouses or significant others. Our rooms need to work just as hard. With this in mind, it's possible to work to bring the whole house together the way you want it to be, rather than have it dictated by the labels we give to various rooms, or by the pictures we see in house magazines. Reclaiming your house to use it the way you live is the ultimate goal. Why go through all the work of renovating and decorating, simply to end up having to put "hands-off" signs on everything? In my own house, while I try to keep my kids from taking grape juice and cookies into the living room, it happens—and the room is set up to accommodate that. My neighbor Kathy just remodeled the first floor of her home, which included eliminating the formal dining room in favor of a much-needed family room that connects to the eat-in kitchen. Recognizing how you

Going Solo

So you want to save money and do some of the work yourself? Great—but before you do, ask yourself a simple question: How much passion have you got for the job?

Like some people, my friends Mike and Judy love to figure things out for themselves. I am amazed at how willing they are to try to do things themselves, and I am always impressed by their spirit. They will dive in and demolish, scrape, patch, and paint just to be part of the process because they love it. And when they've finished one project, they're eager to tackle the next. I always caution people to stay away from do-it-yourself projects that can get them hurt or create a disaster, however. Electrical work comes immediately to mind, as does major plumbing repairs. These are things that are best left to licensed tradespeople. If you love putting things together and being part of the process in other areas, however, be my guest.

If you've got no interest in these things at all other than some vague notion that you can save a few dollars by doing the work yourself, forget it. Your time— and your finances—will be better served elsewhere. Don't view this as a failure, or a sign that you're a bad homeowner. Just the opposite. It shows that you're smart, and that you care about your home.

live, not how you think you should live, is the first step in knowing how to renovate your house.

In terms of décor, the fabrics and the furniture that we choose should all make sense and give us the ability to clean a place up as we use it. We have enough stress in our lives, why compound it by creating rooms that need special protection? Back in the '50s, this was accomplished by wrapping the

An Island Paradise

Kitchen islands make popular room dividers between adjoining family rooms, but the visual clutter can be irritating. After all, who wants to look at all those dirty dishes when entertaining? A good solution to this is to create a two-tiered island, with an ordinary 36-inch-tall countertop on the kitchen side, which steps up to a 42-inch-tall countertop on the family room side. This helps hide the mess from friends and family, and buys you time to do the cleanup when you're ready for it.

furniture entirely in plastic. It's a laughable concept today because of the sheer tackiness, but we often do the equivalent to our whole houses, by creating rooms that can't really be lived in. Instead, let's think beyond the plastic wrapping—whether literal or metaphorical—and come up with rooms and surfaces that don't need such coddling.

One home where I saw this practice at work was in a large condo that an older couple had bought. The luxurious place had four bedrooms, one of which was theirs, one was a guestroom, and one was a home office. The other was empty, but perfectly decorated with new blinds and fresh carpeting, as if it was a project waiting to happen. "What's this room?" I asked. "Oh, that's our 'God Forbid' room," said the woman. "God forbid we should ever need someone to move in here and take care of us, we'll be ready for it." The room gave them peace of mind, knowing that they could look to the future with ease.

That's the sort of planning that makes sense for us all, whether you're retired or just starting a family or anywhere in between. Making your rooms serve you, rather you serving them, is the ultimate goal.

Go with the Flow

My wife, Mary Beth, is not an architect, but she does have a good sense of how a house feels. Sometimes, if we've been to a place, she'll say that she liked it, but that it felt "choppy" inside.

It's true; there is something unsettling about a house where you enter one room, then have to back out of it to leave. A simple task such as finding the kitchen or the bathroom becomes an exercise in discovery and perseverance, like finding your way out of the Minotaur's labyrinth. What's remarkable is that this chopped-up floor plan seems to transcend architectural style. You can find old houses set up this way, as well as new ones. And if you don't already have one, it's all too easy to create one yourself, by going ahead with a botched renovation or an ill-planned addition. This brings me to one simple element

that is the hallmark of a great house. It is not style, nor is it architecture. It has nothing to do with the size of the home or the size of your budget. I can sum it up in two words: circular flow. In a comfortable home, rooms flow from one to another. You walk in one room and out another, rather than bumping into a dead end and having to travel back again.

A Low-Cost Passage

Creating a passageway from one room to another can be an inexpensive solution to a claustrophobic floor plan. Cutting the opening and trimming it might cost $150 in materials if you did it yourself. If you hire a carpenter, the bill might rise to $500. Either way, it's money well spent.

One of my pet peeves is houses where you have to walk through the living room or the dining room to get into the kitchen; this is the style of the old "shotgun" style or "railroad" apartments, so named because the rooms are connected like cars on a train. The result is claustrophobic. I'm a true believer in a hallway or some type of division to show how to get there. This can be accomplished in even the smallest house, as I discovered a few years ago while renovating a tiny American Foursquare, a style of home that was popular a century ago. While I loved the house, I didn't like that you had to walk through the living room and the dining room to get into the kitchen. Worse, when you stepped in through the front door you landed right in the middle of the living room. There was no way to build a full-scale addition, but there were ways to compensate for these shortcomings fairly cheaply. I was able to build out and create a small 6-by-8-foot entryway to create a better landing area. One opening led to the living room, and I was able to create a second opening that led right into the kitchen. The awkward floor plan was solved.

At the same time, I found a way to make some important changes in the combined living room and the dining room. As they existed, the two rooms were a muddle with no real distinction between them other than the furniture. The couch was on the living room side, along with the coffee

A Room That Flexes

Rooms come and go in fashion, from the Florida Room to the Great Room, and the choice these days is the Flex Room.

No, we're not talking a body-building emporium. This is a room that "flexes" because it gives you many options. A Bonus Room is so named because it's extra space, typically above the garage, but this is a marginal area, to say the least. A Flex Room, however, is prime terrain, and one that allows you to do many things over the course of your home ownership. The room can start out as a playroom for the children when they're young, then graduate to a study or computer area as they get older. As the years go by it can become an exercise room or a home office, the choice is yours. The point is, the room can change according to the needs of your family, rather than forcing you to change to a different house.

table and TV set; the dining room table was on the other side. That's how you knew where you were. Instead, it was possible to better define these spaces with some simple additions, rather than partitioning them with a solid wall. Across the ceiling I built a thin soffit, which looked like a finished beam to mark the separation between the two rooms without building a wall. At each end of the soffit I added a pair of architectural columns, which stood about 6 inches away from the wall. The columns and the archway probably cost all of $300 in materials, but they added a great deal more in terms of defining the floor plan and making the rooms seem better planned. These are the sorts of changes you can make that greatly improve your home's livability, without costing a fortune.

Putting It Together

Okay, so you have a plan—now who do you get to do all the work? Unless you're planning on nothing more than some simple painting, a room renovation likely will involve working with a contractor. As everyone who has ever owned a home well knows, this sounds much easier than it actually is. There are the expected aggravations to manage such as delays and cost overruns. Then there are the unexpected ones, such as shoddy workmanship and even criminal billing practices. Being a contractor myself, I can offer a few insights into the Byzantine world of contracting that may help you better manage the process. This will be of use whether you're working on one room or attempting a whole-house makeover.

First, let's take a look at the contracting industry as a whole. Each year, a major consumer research firm conducts a satisfaction survey—or rather a dissatisfaction survey—to find out which profession people find most annoying. Although the order changes from year to year, the top three professions vying for this dubious distinction are invariably lawyers, car salesmen, and home contractors. While I'm not exactly sure why this is, I do have a theory: Contractors make the list because homeowners have a fundamental misunderstanding of what the profession is all about. In addition, homeowners and contractors inhabit entirely different corners of the universe. For a homeowner, renovating a house is most often a labor of love. For a contractor, it's a business deal. As a homeowner, you can learn to

The $64,000 Question

When choosing a general contractor, ask who will actually be doing the work. Is it a group of subcontractors that have been together for years, or is it a brand new collection of workers? The less experienced the contractor, the more likely there will be delays and cost overruns.

Lien and Mean

Building and renovating is largely a matter of trust, until the payment comes due. Then it's essential to pay on time. If you don't pay contractors, you'll get more than a "payment due" notice in a pink envelope. Instead, they'll file a lien against your house, and can take legal action to claim it. Things can get much worse than this, however, since you're also responsible for the bills that your contractors and sub-contractors are supposed to pay. You might have a foundation guy pour the concrete and pay him, thinking you're squared away. But if he didn't in turn pay the concrete company for providing him with the concrete, they can attach a lien to your house to try to collect for the concrete that's sitting under your house. To me, this scenario is scarier than *Nightmare on Elm Street.*

The way to protect yourself from all of this is by requiring everyone to give you copies of their lien waivers, when you pay them for the work performed. Although you may never have heard of it, it's a standard form that everyone in the construction business should be familiar with. If you hire a contractor, they will take care of this for you. But if you contract the work yourself, it's a good idea to stock up on these forms and do them yourself. Lien waivers can be purchased from any office supply store, and a package of ten might cost you all of $5.

manage this arrangement, but first some more details are needed on what exactly a contractor does.

To begin, there are many different kinds of contractors out there, beginning with the ones that are trained in a specific trade. These include plumbers, electricians, heating and cooling specialists, masons, and painters. Think of them the way you would members of an orchestra, each of whom brings an important voice into the mix, but none of whom is able to carry off an entire symphony alone. For this, you need a conductor, or, as they are better known in the home improvement business, a general contractor or "G.C."

With the contractor in charge, the other tradespeople come to work

If you're contracting a large job—say one that costs $100,000 or more, which is the size of a decent-sized addition to your home—there's an even better idea. In this case, hire a title company to make the payments for you. You give the company the cash for the project in advance, which they hold in escrow. Then, when the various workers have finished their jobs, they will be paid by the title company, which will assure that the lien waivers are signed. Since the money is in escrow, the contractors you hire will be far more willing to work without being paid in advance, since they know the money is already there and will be available to them when they've earned it. In fact, they'll be far more willing to work for you, period, because they will respect you as a professional when it comes to your finances.

On a project of this size, the title company might charge you $500 to manage the payments in this way. This is a small price to pay to be assured at the end of this project, when your home is remodeled and finished, that it's yours free and clear of any liens.

on your home as subcontractors or "subs." They're not actually employees of the contractor, in most cases. Instead, they tend to have a long-standing relationship with the contractor, and show up on job after job. The measure of a good contractor is the steadiness of this band of workers. I like to consider myself a reasonably good contractor, and I have worked almost exclusively with the same group of subcontractors for the last decade. A cohesive group of workers offers the possibility for consistency and timeliness in the work that is being done. After all, we've had years and years together to sort out all of our weaknesses and take advantage of each other's strengths. The result is a job that will turn out more or less on budget and with predictable high quality. There's a relationship among the members in this group that's based on trust, and having a trusting relationship is what business is all about.

I would like to emphasize the word "business" because this is what homeowners most often fail to understand—that they're entering into a business relationship. Instead, they mistakenly think of it as a friendly relationship, and believe that everyone working on their home will see it in this same way. I have news for you. A general contractor is not getting involved in your project because he really wants to help you; he's coming over and assembling his crew because he's figured out a way to make a bigger profit from you than from any other projects he's currently considering. I don't mean to be crass. Sure, contractors can be great people and working with them can be a rewarding experience. But by failing to

Proof Positive

Let's say you hire someone to do some work on your house. Perhaps a handyman arrives to clean the gutters. Then he accidentally slips and falls off the ladder, which is terrible for him—and even worse for you, because he doesn't carry his own insurance and sues you.

Granted, we all pay a lot of attention to insurance that applies to ourselves. But how many of us think about insurance that applies to contractors and subcontractors working in our homes? Probably very few. The reality is, however, that anyone hurt on the job at your home can sue you, unless the contractor that hires them carries adequate insurance policies. Notice I said policies, because there are several types of insurance involved here, from liability insurance to builder's risk insurance, that are essential for proper coverage. Without these, you can be sued for medical bills, lost wages, and more. This is the dark side of contracting that few people think about when choosing between the $15-an-hour handyman who carries no insurance, and the $35-an-hour one who works for a fully licensed contractor. Or the "plumber" who will install a new water heater for $250, and the licensed, insured plumber who will charge $1,000.

How do you know who's insured and who's not? Ask. Then ask for proof. Any recognize the stark business aspect of this relationship, homeowners can get into real trouble, as I will detail in a moment.

I've always likened being a general contractor to being like Clint Eastwood in the old TV show, *Rawhide*. You have to ride the cattle herd hard as you're crossing the plains. Only in this case, those cattle are all the subcontractors. You're trying to get them all to go in one direction—namely, the completion of the project—but instead they're under all sorts of pressures to stray. "Ooh," a plumber might say. "I can make a fast $500 by changing out a water heater at another job, so I'll be back tomorrow." If that happens, the entire job slows to a halt while everyone waits for the plumber to return. Then it's like a giant domino effect. Since the plumber isn't finished on time, the electrician can't start, and takes another job to

contractor or worker who carries insurance will be able to show you a certificate granted by their insurance company that proves they have coverage. You should expect to see liability coverage of at least $1 million per occurrence, and you should request to be listed as additionally insured. Your name will literally appear right there on the insurance certificate. Contractors should also have workman's compensation insurance on all their employees.

Any contractors worth their tool belts will give you all this information without a second thought. If they blink, look elsewhere. And don't let them start before you see all the documents. If they balk by telling you the policy is in the mail, the chances are they don't have insurance at all, which could leave you holding the bill if anything goes wrong.

Eight Rules of General Contracting

When trying to save money on a major project, many homeowners decide to become their own general contractors in order to get the job done. To help out, here are a few things I've discovered along the way:

1. Be confident in knowing that as you're successful, you will end up creating new relationships with fine, hardworking people who you'll be able to recommend to your friends and family.

2. Know that you'll learn more about home renovation and remodeling than you ever dreamed, and will inevitably become the neighborhood expert. In the same way that everyone tells a doctor at a cocktail party about all their ailments, expect to be consulted about everything from leaky pipes to drafty windows.

3. Be motivated by the knowledge that you'll have a huge sense of accomplishment in working on the project. You'll have assumed the role of leader for a group of contractors, and can claim a principal role in leading the project to completion.

4. Know that this will be one of the most exhausting, as well as one of the most rewarding, things you've ever done. You will be happy, you will be sad, you

keep busy that will pull him away for an additional week. And without the electrician's work done, the carpenter can't finish the interior work, and takes a "quick" kitchen installation someplace else. Before you know it, the subcontractors are scattered over the Great Plains of the home improvement landscape, and your job site remains as vacant as some abandoned little house on the prairie.

Do they care about your pleas and even tears as a homeowner to get the job finished, so that you can get on with your life? No, they do not. Because this is a business proposition to them. They have to make money every single day they work. And if there are any hiccups in the schedule, they can't wait around for things to be sorted out; instead, they fly to another job to will cry, you will laugh. And when it's all done, you'll probably be itching to start another project.

5. Know that success lies in choosing the right people to work on your home, and in building relationships that allow you to get answers that you can trust.

6. You'll spend twice as much time managing things as you could predict. Make sure you factor this in to the process. Most of us have full-time jobs, which makes this the equivalent of moonlighting.

7. Never forget that this is a business proposition as far as the contractors are concerned. Although you're emotionally attached to the job—it is, after all, your home—force yourself to put on a different hat and run the project like a business.

8. Know that the broom is as mighty as the hammer. A clean site creates better working conditions for contractors, and is a lot easier to live with for your family. At the end of the day, make sure you sweep up and vacuum as much as possible, even if you expect another mess the next day.

be paid. If the carpenter doesn't show up on a Monday, the painters might suddenly bolt for another job on Tuesday, and not return until Saturday. As a result, everything gets pushed back, not just days but even multiple days or multiple weeks. The general contractor may have done everything possible to keep the herd from straying, but they're gone.

This is where general contractors that work with the same group of subcontractors all the time have an advantage. They're better at keeping the herd together. Because they guarantee work to the subcontractors year in and year out, they can be demanding and set a schedule that the subcontractors will respect. Does the wiring need to be done by Wednesday? Believe me, it will get done. Does the painting have to be completed by Saturday? The painters may stay up all night getting it accomplished, but they will. And the reason they will is because they've worked with the general contractor for a decade. The G.C. pays bills on time, and the subcontractors can count on working on a dozen projects or more over the course of any given year. For them, it's the equivalent of signing up for a frequent flier program.

Saving Money?

While many people try to become their own general contractors for a major project in order to save money, they often end up spending more than if they hired a professional in the first place. This is because subcontractors usually give a general contractor a better rate, sort of like a bulk discount. Homeowners, by contrast, can expect to pay retail prices wherever they go.

For anyone who thinks they can save money by becoming their own general contractor on a project, the problem should be obvious by now. The odds that you can get people to show up when you need them are against you. That's because you're a one-time deal to them. The chances of that painter or that electrician or that plumber ever working for you again are slim, and they know this. You may call up a plumber weeks in advance and schedule them for a particular Monday, and think that everything will run smoothly. But then, late Sunday night, they get a call from a general contractor who builds ten houses a year, and needs them the next day for an emergency job. Guess where the plumber will be headed when he wakes up? If you guessed to the contractor's job, advance token to "Go." As long as you understand these rules, you can appreciate why good contractors tend to charge so much money. And if you choose to go it alone, you can better appreciate what the number one virtue to cultivate will be: patience.

Now that we've gone through the basics of layout and contracting, let's take a look at a single room and explore the floor-to-ceiling possibilities for a makeover.

chapter TWO

Room for Improvement
What can you do to make a single room better? First, look beneath that coat of paint.

Sometimes the problem with a house isn't in its layout or style or sense of proportion. The problem lies in the deteriorated condition of the rooms themselves.

This was the situation encountered by an acquaintance of mine named Tony. He moved into a two-family house in Staten Island, New York, and took the first-floor apartment for himself. The house was a grand, if tired-looking, Queen Anne beauty built in the 1880s. He rebuilt the front porch and reshingled everything in the original pattern, and the exterior looked perfect. One step inside, however, and everything seemed wrong, beginning in the living room. All the elements of a grand space were there—a fireplace, thick crown molding and baseboard trim, antique fir floors—but in a serious form of decay. It had all the appeal of a college dorm room, last renovated in about 1910. There wasn't any one element that needed to be changed; the problem was that the whole room need-ed to be redone. Rather than just slapping a coat of paint on everything, however, Tony set to work. He stripped paint from the woodwork, hired someone to redo the floors, installed new windows that resembled the old ones, and carefully smoothed the walls and ceiling. When it was fin-

Floors Galore

In the effort to unify a house and make it appear to have a floor plan that allows a smoother traffic floor, don't fail to notice the single most important element right beneath your feet: the flooring.

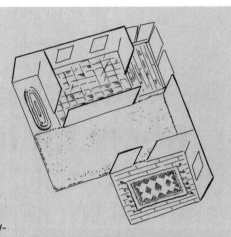

A consistent flooring throughout a house can make things seem well-planned and logical. Too often, however, houses have floor surfaces that change from room to room. You might find slate in the entry hall, red oak in the hallway, cherry in the living room, and Mexican tiles in the kitchen. The result is a patchwork of colors and textures that makes the house look more like a crazy quilt than a well-planned home. It's jarring to the eyes, and jangling to the nerves to live with.

Instead, I'm an advocate of keeping the flooring consistent from one room to another, to bring all the elements of design together. This doesn't have to pigeonhole you to one particular look for every room either, since you can accent certain rooms with area rugs or smaller carpets for contrast. But the effect of a unified flooring is powerful, and goes a long way toward preventing a house from looking choppy.

ished and carefully painted, the room looked worthy of the home's grand exterior. "Every little detail matters," said Tony, with real pride.

There is no shortage of home makeover projects on TV shows and in magazines. But when you take a close look at what these involve, you'll discover that most of them focus on paint and décor alone. If a room is crumbling, you paint it, add new furniture and drapes, decorate it with some tchotchkes, and call it a makeover. That looks fine for a quick photo shoot, perhaps, but not if you're living with a home. Your eye as the homeowner will inevitably focus on the parts that aren't quite so pristine:

the windows that don't work, the woodwork glopped with decades of paint, the floor with the broken pieces of wood.

Instead of rushing through yet another paint job, I'd like to focus on how to give a room the makeover it really needs, before a single coat of paint goes on. Let's begin with the floors.

What Lies Beneath

Searching for a home with my wife some years back, we stumbled on a brick Georgian that had been built in 1941 and was still occupied by the original owner. The home had carpeting everywhere, most of which looked like it, too, was installed in 1941. Stepping to a corner of one room, I saw the carpeting was a bit loose, and pulled it back to reveal beautiful red-oak floors beneath it. When we closed on the house, I went there the very first day and ripped out every piece of carpeting to expose the most beautiful floors I had seen—void of knots, wide, and lovely. Other than replacing a few boards where someone's fish tank had leaked decades earlier, all we had to do was have the floors sanded, and they looked like new.

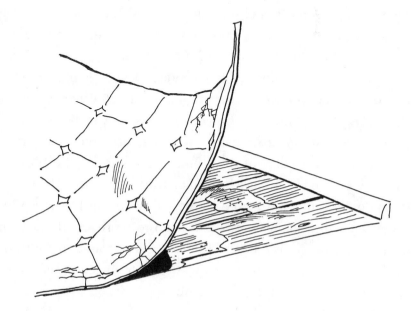

Time for a New Wood Floor?

Wood floors are amazingly renewable, but even this remarkable material has its limits. Each time a floor is sanded, it takes about ⅛ of an inch of wood with it. Wood floorboards are typically only ¾ of an inch thick, however. This means that after three or four sandings, the wood will likely be so thin that the tongue-and-groove sections holding it together will be visible. The only choice at this point is to replace them. A good flooring contractor will be able to tell you whether you've got enough wood to work with—before you spend the money to have a floor refinished.

To me, the floor is the dominant feature of any room, and should be the first focus on any room makeover. More than just a surface to walk on, it's the surface that gives great texture and color to a room. Except for the floors in the bathroom and kitchen, the overwhelming majority of floors are wood, so let's discuss the basics of restoring this most beautiful of materials. Wood floors are probably the most renewable and malleable surface around. The real beauty of wood is that it can literally be reborn when approached the right way. Not just fixed up a little bit, but fixed up a lot. Let's look at some of the possibilities.

The quest to make a floor look new again begins with a close examination of the floorboards. A professional floor refinisher will do more than simply turn on the sander and get to work. Any nail holes and missing splinters of wood are repaired with stainable putty or putty that closely matches the color of the wood. Sometimes, entire boards will need to be replaced if they are broken or water-damaged. There are two ways to do this, and I'll describe the wrong way first: This involves cutting out the segments of boards that need to be replaced, then simply nailing new pieces in as a patch. The result is a "trap door" effect, that looks exactly like what it is—a sloppy attempt to finish off the floor, collect a check, and rush on to the next job.

Unless you're planning to cover the area permanently with an area rug, there is a far better way. And that is to "tooth" the new boards in. In this way, the damaged boards are removed from the entire length, not just cut out in the area to be patched. Then, new boards are actually worked into the existing floor to exactly mimic the spacing of the original boards. When this is done correctly and the boards are sanded and finished, the result will be a patch that is invisible. Now, where do you get the pieces of wood that you need to replace the missing ones? This takes some creativity. Pieces can be pulled from an out-of-the-way area, such as inside a closet or perhaps an old bathroom that is going to be tiled. If

A Heat Register with Class

Sometimes, it's the little things that make a house look well finished. One such example is the floor ducts in a house with a forced-air heating system. Usually these are rectangular metal vents, with an industrial look. In my home, however, I exchanged these for vents made from hardwood that match the flooring.

These might cost about $30 to $40 per vent, and come in any number of species, from oak to maple, that can be stained and finished to match the wood. They almost disappear, except when someone looks at them closely. I have three registers done in wood in my living room, and I can't tell you how many times people have commented on them as we stand there talking. The best part about these is that they can be added easily to an existing floor. A flooring contractor—or you, if you're handy—can remove the old vents, cut the area to the size of the new one, then nail and putty it in place. Finished properly, it will look as if it's always been there.

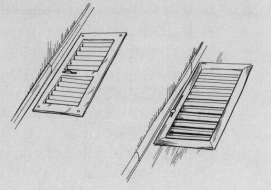

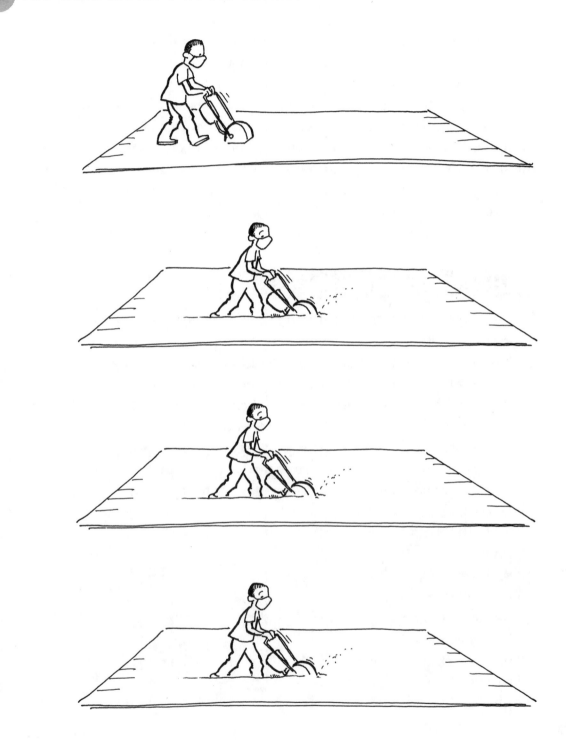

you can't find spare pieces of wood in the house, know that most of the flooring you'll likely encounter is still available at a lumberyard. Whether it's white oak, maple, red oak, or walnut, you'll be able to find what you're looking for with a simple search. The great thing about wood is that no matter what sort of patina it has from age, it will look brand new once it's sanded, so all the pieces should match. If they don't, you can stain the entire floor, which will tie everything together, old and new.

Once the floor has been puttied and patched, it's time for the next step. The key to refinishing a wood floor is to have it sanded down. This literally removes the top surface of the wood, and exposes a raw, fresh surface lying just beneath. No matter how weathered or worn-looking a piece of wood might be, removing the surface will expose wood beneath it that looks like it came right out of the mill. The challenge is to do the sanding correctly. Many homeowners make a mistake, however, in thinking that they can do this themselves. Wrong. Finishing a wood floor ranks up there with the greatest skills, such as building a custom fireplace mantel or fabricating granite countertops. No matter how handy you may feel, resist the temptation to run out and rent a floor sander to attempt the job yourself. Not only do you risk botching up the finish, you risk botching up the actual flooring itself, in the form of indelible ridges and even sander-shaped holes in the wood that will require new flooring to repair.

The problem lies in the fact that equipment available to homeowners is sub-par. Whatever you can find to rent at the local home improvement center will simply not be up to the task of excellent work. Professionals, by contrast, have much larger commercial units that run off 240-volt electrical connections, which are similar to the outlets that an electric dryer runs from. When floor refinishers come into your home with their equipment, they won't even bother trying to plug it into an outlet; they'll wire it directly into the electric service panel to get the enormous floor of energy they need. What do they do with all this extra power? It goes to supply the motor of the commercial-grade sanders to keep it spinning at a consistently high rate. Professional-grade machines bite evenly into the

Give Your Floors a Facelift

Wood floors are a beautiful, and greatly valued, feature of any house. Just take a look at any real estate listings to see what I mean. You'll see "hardwood floors throughout" listed right up there with granite countertops and three-car garages. Inevitably, however, the finish on these floors becomes tired looking—not worn-out enough to warrant a complete refinishing, but certainly in need of some cosmetic overhauling. What can be done?

The answer can be found in a number of products that fall under the category of "floor rejuvenators," for want of a better term. One brand is called Renewal, manufactured by Varathane, and another is Hardwood Floor Refresher by Bona X. These restore the sheen and look of your floors, without having to go through the expense of refinishing them. The products work like this: Wash and carefully dry the floors, then mop on the waterborne finish. I've found a synthetic sheepskin pad works best. The rejuvenator hides most of the small scratches on the floor, and goes on in a very manageable way. One thing to keep in mind is that you have to do the whole floor. Doing one patch will simply call out the area too much, just as if you only polished the scuff marks on your shoes.

Take note about one thing, however. If you've got deep gouges in the floor, even a floor rejuvenator can't help. Instead, you have to first mask a scratch that goes into raw wood with a touch-up crayon for wood, which is available at any home improvement center.

surface of the wood, without bogging down or overloading as the machine is moved, which is what prevents waviness in a sanded floor. These powerful machines glide along the surface, leaving a perfectly smooth plane of wood in their wake. I've seen homeowners again and again make the mistake of trying to rent the equipment themselves, only to end up with flooring that would probably look better covered up with linoleum.

While you shouldn't attempt this yourself, knowing how a floor is refinished will help you know whether the contractors you hire are doing the job correctly. When sanding a floor they typically make three passes with the machine. The first pass is done with a 60-grit sandpaper, which is a material so coarse it looks as if pebbles have been thrown on it. They then graduate to a much finer 100-grit paper, and a third pass with a paper somewhere in the range of 120 to 160 grit. Over the course of this, probably ⅛ of an inch of wood is removed.

It's All in the Finish

With the wood floors revitalized, it's time to turn our attention to finishing the newly sanded surfaces. I would like to begin by making a bold statement: I love stained-wood floors.

While wood floors finished in a clear, natural finish have a traditional look, I think stain brings out an additional element of depth and character. This is true with new or old floors, but it has an especial advantage with old floors since the stain helps to hide imperfections. Those hundreds of holes that have to be puttied where the linoleum or carpeting

New Floors vs. Resurfacing

Refinishing floors is expensive—between $1.50 and $2.50 per square foot, not including any repairs needed or boards replaced. But with new floors costing between $6 to $8 a square foot, it ranks as one of the great bargains in home improvement.

had been fastened, for instance, disappear under a coat of light stain. Any patched floorboards, too, will disappear seamlessly into the rows of floorboards. Stained floors also have a warmth and a patina that is more characteristic of an older home, rather than the stark bright surface of unstained wood.

The trick in staining floors successfully is to test out the colors first. As with anything, the color you see on the sample chart may look entirely different when rubbed into the floor in front of you. To help you make a selection, professional floor finishers will do stain samples right on the floor. They will put down areas of dark, medium, and light stains, and let you see how it looks up against the trim and walls. When you've made your choice, they then make a quick pass over the test patches with a sander to eliminate them, then apply the color you choose. One thing to keep in mind is that oil-based stains don't dry, they cure. This means that even though they may look dry and feel dry a few minutes after being applied, they are not. Any finished coat laid on top of an uncured stained surface will begin to lift and flake off over time. As a rule of thumb, the darker the stain, the longer it will take to cure. If you go with a light color, such as golden oak, it will probably take a full day to cure. But if you use a darker color such as walnut, you're going to have to wait two and probably even three days before the final finish goes down.

For the final finish coat on floors, I'm a big fan of waterborne finishes, as opposed to oil-based finishes. The reason is that these tend to dry to

Safe Stripping

If you live in an old house with wide molding around windows and doorways, you'll notice that the detail is often lost to about one hundred years' worth of paint. Removing this is a laborious, aggravating job, made worse because many of the chemicals used in stripping paint can be hugely toxic. Sanding the surfaces and burning the paint off can be even worse, because of the risk of filling your home with toxic lead from the old paint.

One of the better products I've had some luck with is a product called Citrus Strip. This is exactly what it sounds like: It's made from concentrated citrus oils, and smells something like oranges. While it's not as aggressive as other chemical strippers, it's also not as noxious. You can safely use it indoors and continue to stay there while it works. This stripper won't remove as many layers of paint in one application as some of the other brands, but it does do a good job if you're patient. And when it comes to stripping paint, patience is the key ingredient.

Not satisfied with the slow and steady approach? A quicker alternative is to literally remove the trim from the interior of your home, and ship it to a commercial paint stripper to have the job done for you. A commercial stripper will soak the pieces of wood in a giant vat of chemicals and make quick work of what to you would be a lengthy operation. I have a few words of caution about this, however. First, make sure you carefully label the pieces of wood with an indelible marker so that everything can be fit back together again when it returns. Second, I would not recommend having doors dipped in stripper, since the chemicals have a tendency to dissolve the glues that hold the various layers of veneer and door panels together. And, finally, know that even though you're having your trim quick-dipped, you'll still have some work to do. The stripping process raises the grain in the wood, and you'll have to lightly sand it before painting or sealing it.

a harder surface because of the acrylic resins they contain, compared to the oil-based alternatives. In addition, waterborne finishes tend not to yellow over time, which can truly detract from the look of a wood floor, especially one that is unstained. Waterborne fin-

All or Nothing

Anyone who tries to refinish one small patch of a floor is going to be disappointed, because the area will stand out markedly in sheen and color from the rest of the floor. If a portion of a floor needs to be refinished, the whole floor needs to be refinished.

ishes are much more user-friendly since the odor they release is minimal. They can also be recoated more quickly. While you may have to wait twenty-four hours or more before applying a second coat of an oil-based finish, you can recoat a waterborne finish in as little as two hours. For products, I prefer the commercial brands that are used in heavily trafficked places such as shopping malls, restaurants, and even bowling alleys. One product is made by a Swedish company called BonaKemi, and another is called Street Shoe, made by Basic Coatings, Inc. While you may not find these in the average home improvement centers, you'll certainly find them through hardwood flooring distributors.

Now comes another big question: How many coats of finish should a floor get? More than you think. A floor finisher I work with named Peter is adamant about his recipe for floors—and with the consistently high-quality results he gets, he has every reason to be.

The first coat of finish, he says, is called the seal coat, because it literally sinks right into the wood and seals the surface. After spreading this coat on with a synthetic sheepskin pad, he lets it dry for a couple of hours. Then he moves in with a giant circular buffing machine to which he attaches a buffing pad that resembles a porch screen. This is similar to the machines that you see being used late nights in a grocery store. Rather than sanding the floor, the screen lightly abrades any wood fibers that have absorbed the seal coat and popped up above the surface. It is not rough enough to gouge into the wood and remove the stain, however.

When the floor is smooth, he vacuums it, and then gives it another coat. This is followed by more screening and more vacuuming. Now Peter is ready for the third, and final, coat. Since this is the layer you'll see, the sheen level is important to consider. Like paints, most floor coatings come in various sheens, from matte and semigloss to high gloss. I avoid high-gloss finishes in houses, because they tend to be too shiny and also tend to highlight any scratches or imperfections that occur over time. Instead, I prefer semigloss, which has a rich sheen yet is more forgiving to live with.

If the floor finishers are smart, they'll turn off any central air conditioning or forced-hot air system you have in your home as they work, in order to reduce the amount of airborne particles that can settle on the wet finish. When the floor is finished, it's important that you listen to them as far as when you can safely walk on it. Typically, the finish dries in two hours, but you will want to make sure that you're not walking on that floor for a good four to six hours, and then be sure to do so only in your socks. Although it feels dry, the finish is still curing, and even though the layer on the top is hard, it is still curing underneath and could be soft. This is just like going to Dairy Queen and having a vanilla cone dipped in chocolate: The shell is hard on the outside, but the inside is soft. In most cases, you want to give it at least forty-eight hours before you put your shoes on and before you start putting furniture back in place.

To further protect your new floor finish and keep it from scratching, you have to be rigorous about putting felt pads on the bottom of every piece of furniture you have. If you don't, the floor will become scratched in no time. These pads have either an adhesive backing that sticks on the legs of your table of chair, or a small metal ring that you actually pound in to the bottoms of the legs. Stay away from the ones tapped in with a single nail, however. I've found that as the felt pad wears, which it inevitably will, it exposes the nail and scratches the floor.

Home Is Where the Hearth Is

The fireplace tends to be one of those features of a home we think is fixed and unchanging, but in fact a lot can be done to alter it. Adding a new mantel or new tiles to surround it can result in a fireplace that is literally reborn. There are so many different options and products and materials and colors and choices, it boggles the mind. Many fireplace or patio stores will have brand new units that you can purchase, or if you're a bit more of a sleuth, you can find an architectural salvage store. These are common in big cities, and specialize in stocking beautiful old mantels and other fireplace pieces from old buildings. These can be modified to fit just about any fireplace opening in any home.

If you've got an old brick fireplace in a home, the mantel tends to be something that is built in around the existing masonry. To change this,

It's a Gas

While I always fancied myself as a wood-only guy where the fireplace is concerned, I've had a change of heart with my current house. We've switched to gas, and there's no switching back for me.

Starting a fire used to involve a ten-minute visit to the wood pile to split wood, most of which was damp. Then, like everyone else who isn't an Eagle Scout, I would spend another ten minutes trying to get the wood to light. This usually involved filling the house with giant puffs of caustic smoke. Now, however, I walk over to the fireplace, press a button, and there's an instant fire. No smoke, no exertion, and no ashes to scoop out.

I used to think gas log kits were as tacky as plastic beams, but they've come a long way and are now astonishingly realistic. You can even choose them in authentic-looking "species" of wood, such as oak or birch. A high-quality gas fireplace log kit might cost $600 to $1,000 and about another $120 to install, assuming you already have a gas supply to your home. This makes a great upgrade in any home with a fireplace.

you may have to rip everything out and expose some of the rough masonry that's underneath. Clearly, this is more than a weekend project, but it can be done. The new mantel fits right into the space occupied by the old one, and then everything is covered back up again. You may have to install some additional trim or do some additional work to make it all fit together. When it's done, it will certainly require painting or staining. Despite the labor, the project can be more than worth the effort. A renewed fireplace can become the centerpiece of a revived room, and make a huge difference in how it looks.

And what if you don't have a fireplace at all? They've never been easier to add. Adding a fireplace used to require building a brick chimney, but new ones can be installed as prefabricated metal boxes. These are fully insulated to reduce any fire risk, and require only a one-inch separation from anything combustible. This means you can literally put them in a living room one inch away from the wall, then frame around it to give it a built-in look. Wood-burning fireplaces do need to be vented outside, of course, either through a chimney or a galvanized-metal stack specially designed for fireplaces. If you go for a gas fireplace, however, the installation is much easier. Instead of having to be vented up a chimney, the gas fireplace simply needs to be vented out to the exterior wall, and, in some cases, doesn't need to be vented at all. These operate similar to a gas stove, and vent directly into the room. While these don't look exactly like a real fireplace, they come fairly close, especially when fitted with a beautiful mantel and surrounded with tile, brick, or stone veneer.

Walls and Ceilings

Walls and ceilings are strange in one respect. In a room that is otherwise crumbling—with floors that need refinishing and windows rattling loose—they're hardly noticed. Yet suddenly, when the windows are fixed, the floors refinished, and the woodwork stripped of one hundred years of paint, the walls and ceilings stand out as in desperate need of attention. Every crack, every wave, every imperfection becomes magnified.

The proper work in smoothing things over here will help lay a strong foundation for the décor to come in Chapter 3. Preparation is 90 percent of the paint job—rather, make that 99 percent of the job. The effort spent here will be well worth it.

The goal is to make the walls as smooth as possible, which can be a laughable

Time to Say Good-bye?

Plaster is a great material, but it does have a definite limit to its life span. If you have continually appearing cracks that defy repair, or large chunks of plaster that feel loose or sound hollow when knocked on, you've got trouble. The solution lies in removing all the loose material, and starting over again with either plaster or drywall.

goal if you take a close look at the walls in many houses. But it can be achieved. I've seen walls that have more bumps and ripples than a 3-D map of the United States finish beautifully, and the same can be achieved in your home. There are two common surfaces, plaster and drywall. Let's focus on plaster first.

Plaster has its great virtues: It's practically soundproof, hard, durable, and a great surface for painting. That is, until it cracks. This is inevitable, especially as an old house settles. Plaster cracks have a magical quality, in that they absolutely defy patching. You can smooth the cracks over with joint compound, and sand the wall perfectly smooth. Then, within a few days, the cracks will appear again. You could patch a crack a thousand times this way, and it will still appear. I know you don't want to hear this, but the only true solution for a crack in a plaster wall is to literally cut into the wall, create a larger opening, take out all the broken material, and either repatch the area with new plaster or use drywall to create a patch with a different material. The key for this to be effective is to cut the plaster out so that the new hole extends all the way from one stud in the wall to the next, which is where the stress area is. This can be time consuming, as well as messy, but you don't want to take all this effort with these rooms and end up being incensed every time you look at a crack.

While drywall doesn't have the hard surface or the soundproofing qualities of plaster, it is popular because of its low cost and relative ease of installation. It's easy to install, that is, if you know what you're doing. If you don't, hanging drywall for the first time can make you feel like Lucy in the chocolate factory; it's more complicated than it might seem at first and the result can be a huge mess. Drywall comes in large sheets of varying sizes. Done correctly, these come together to form a smooth plane on the walls and ceiling. Done incorrectly, however, the joints show, which gives everything a cobbled-together look. Worse, the screws used to hold the drywall in place begin to pop out slightly, and the tape used to seal the joints begins to peel away from the wall. A botched drywall installation can make a room look worse than some package from UPS left out in the rain.

Fortunately, a botched drywall installation can be easily corrected by a professional painter—without having to go back in and do the drywall over again. The wall can be sanded smooth with a power sander

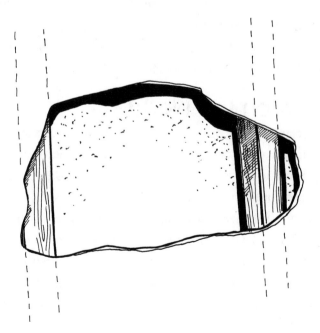

It's All in the Tools

Patching and smoothing drywall with joint compound is a job that requires the right tools. Professionals use large spatulas, ranging in width from 6 to 12 inches. They begin using the narrower tools, then gradually work up to wider and wider ones. This smoothes out the joint compound over the patches, and makes it flow imperceptibly into the rest of the wall or ceiling. By contrast, many homeowners try to spread on joint compound with a 1-inch putty knife. Good luck: The result will be a surface filled with so many bumps and ridges it will resemble moguls on a ski run.

specially designed for drywall. New joint compound, which is the plaster-like material used to cover screw holes and hide joints, can be feathered over the cracks. Any holes greater than an inch or so can be repaired by using small pieces of drywall, which are held in place by mesh tape and then covered with joint compound. In really bad situations, every wall and ceiling can literally be coated with a smooth ⅛-inch-thick layer of joint compound, then sanded to perfection. The result will be a surface that looks like plaster, and hides the imperfections of the drywall beneath it.

A Window on the World

Windows are crucial to a room, both in bringing in light and in keeping the elements under control. Here, you have three options for managing windows: upgrading them, replacing them, and adding new ones in entirely different configurations.

First, keep in mind that nearly all windows can be renovated rather than replaced. This is especially important with older houses, where the windows themselves form an important part of the architecture. In my own house, the dining room and living room had a total of eight classic French windows that, when opened, turned the rooms into what felt like screened-in porches. I had never seen windows like these before, and although we replaced all the other windows in the house, we chose to salvage these. While this may seem like an environmentally-friendly procedure—since we ended up not sending eight windows to the land-fill and buying eight others—there is another balance sheet to keep in mind, which is the energy that is lost through drafty windows. By replacing windows, in most cases, you'll be saving money on your energy bills.

The window replacement business is a very large industry, with a lot of not only misinformation, but confusing information. The quick answer to finding suitable replacements is to let price be your guide. In general, if something seems cheap, it probably is cheap for a reason. You can buy no-name windows and have them installed for under $300 per opening, but these won't ultimately add any real value to your home. By contrast, buy windows from respected manufacturers, such as Marvin, Pella, or Anderson, and you'll be doing yourself a favor. Not only do these companies make great windows, but they will also add to your home's desirability. The cost is higher—perhaps $500 or even $600 per window or more, including the cost of the installation—but the payoff is worth it. I'll argue forever that you should buy the best windows you

Don't Forget the Glass

In addition to the quality of the window frame, the quality of the glass is something to consider. Thermal-pane windows, which contain two or three layers of glass separated by an insulating pocket of air, are essential whether you live in a very hot or very cold climate. A further upgrade to low-emissivity or "low-e" glass can also make sense. This contains an unseen film on the outside that allows light to enter but blocks ultraviolet radiation and reduces the heat flow both in and out. Heat mirror glass is a step up from this; it blocks up to 99 percent of ultraviolet light. It almost does too good a job, however, because it also blocks out some of the visible light and can dim the look of a room.

possibly can. It's something you'll appreciate, and it's something that adds real value to your home when it comes time to sell it.

One way to manage the costs of new window installation is to space the work out, so that you're not doing the entire house all at once. If you're working on the living room, do those windows only, then tackle the others in the future. This allows you to spread out the costs because you're not having to pay to do it all at once. Installing windows is not like cutting the grass, which is something you have to do all at once. Instead, it can proceed on a much slower schedule. You can replace three or four windows in your home this year, a few more next year, and more the year after that, and finally, four or five years later, you've got it all done. The windows you installed five years ago are of no less value than the ones you installed this year, as long as you choose high-quality windows.

Adding more windows, and not just replacing them, is the key to many successful renovations. There's no magic formula for adding them, but careful attention to the possibilities will help you create a great space. Installing a new window is hardly a drastic project, especially for a good carpenter. The cost of installing a top-quality window and finishing the wall inside and out might range from $700 to $1,200, which, in the scheme of things, is not a huge percentage of a renovation budget. This also gives you a chance to think beyond the rectangle. The typical casement and double-hung windows are fine, but you can bring in more light and actually add more space by installing windows in configurations that jut out from the main room. Bay windows, bow windows, and box windows offer huge opportunities for accomplishing this, at prices that are far cheaper than adding an addition. You might spend $4,000 for a large bay window with a window seat, but compare this to the $20,000 cost of a simple room addition.

Now that we've covered the basics of renovating a room, let's take a look at what to do with it now that it's done—from décor to furniture.

chapter THREE

Décor Galore

Now that you've got the perfect room, it's time to think about decorating and furnishing it.

Sometimes in our haste to make things "look nice," we run the risk of making some major mistakes.

Take my friends Kurt and Lisa, for instance. Used to living in big-city rental apartments, they learned to make creative good use of paint and wallpaper and clever accessories. They thought the same no-frills approach would work for them when they bought a charming though slightly ramshackle 1920s cottage, a few miles from the skyscraper-filled center of Dallas. Working late into the evenings, they spent months decorating everything, including painting and wallpapering every surface, laying carpeting remnants they bought at a discount, and finding furniture for every nook. Just when they thought it was all done, however, they discovered a few problems.

First, a leak in the bathroom turned into a plumbing catastrophe, which involved repairmen bashing through plaster walls to update an antiquated system. Then, a faint burning smell hinted of an overheated wire, and had them rethink the wisdom of continuing on with the ancient cloth-insulated electrical system that coursed through their home. Replacing this involved chiseling through the walls with an electric

41

Painting Walls and Ceilings

In the rush to get things looking good, nothing's easier than slapping on a coat of paint, right? Wrong, wrong, and wrong. Painting, if it's done right, is laborious, time-consuming work. If you're going to do it, be sure to do it right. Here's a quick overview of the steps you'll need to take.

Before applying a single drop of paint, it is essential to make sure that walls and ceilings are well-patched and smooth. You can't cover up cracks and bumpy areas with paint alone, although this seldom stops people from trying. If you look at a surface it might seem smooth. But the professionals take a more rigorous approach. They use bright halogen work lights, and shine them against the surface on an angle to expose any imperfections. Then they patch with joint compound, sand, and patch and repeat the process again and again until the surfaces are smooth. This to me is what "painting" is all about, and why it takes so much time. Cut this stage short, and you might as well not even bother to paint at all.

Now comes the next step, which is also usually forgotten. And that is to wash the walls and ceilings. These surfaces are dirty—which is why we want to paint them in the first place—but you can't simply paint over dirt and expect it to stick.

router to make way for the new electric wiring, which created more dust than a storm in the Sahara. Within a month, nearly everything that they had fixed came undone. "We put the cart before the horse," said Lisa, in characteristic understatement. When the renovation projects were finished a half-year later, they had to begin their painstaking decorating task all over again.

What homeowner doesn't live for the moment when a room gets pulled together, with all its final touches firmly in place? We can't wait to choose paint colors, fabrics for furniture and draperies, and shop for the perfect accent pieces such as a set of side chairs in an antique

Instead, you need to wash the dirt and dust from all that patching with a strong cleaner. I prefer trisodium phosphate, or TSP, and warm water (just remember to wear rubber work gloves, as this cleaner is slightly caustic). After washing the walls, rinse them with clean water and let them dry.

Is it time to paint yet? Not exactly. Now it's time to prime the walls. This is ordinarily a step that people do by instinct on bare drywall, but they rarely prime walls that have already been painted. But priming is essential at this stage, I believe. For one thing, you need to prime the areas that have been sanded and patched. And for another thing, priming gives you a consistent base throughout the room. That way, the finished paint will look even, minus the blotchy spots that mar the work of most homeowners. If you just painted a few years ago do you need to prime again? I would say yes. A shortcut will always be evident.

Now comes the paint. Go ahead and brush on a coat. Then, when it is dry, brush on a second coat. Two coats of paint are essential for a good, durable finish. I know many manufacturers sell "one-coat" paints, but these to me do not work well. The only way to get a truly decent looking wall is to wash it, prime it, and finish it off with two coats of paint.

shop or a handmade lamp that will complete the makeover. After all, these are the surfaces we live with. We're not going to invite anyone over to dinner, then brag and boast about the wonderful new electrical service box that has just been installed in the basement. Guests will, however, look admiringly at the well-tended surfaces and interesting objects around them. These matter, as long as you work on them in the correct order, after first addressing any major structural and mechanical issues.

Assuming you have the essential systems of a room in place, let's take a trip through the basics of home decorating. While I am no Martha

Stewart-in-a-tool-belt, I have listened in on enough decorators doing their jobs to be able to divulge more than a few of their secrets to help you create a beautiful, and livable, home.

A Primer on Color

I had a friend who began each stage of decorating by consulting the paint color charts. Swept up by the poetry of the color names while working on his living room—from "Autumn Mist" to "Raspberry Cream"—he clearly lost his bearings. When finished, he went for what he thought was a neutral color called "Pearl Harbor," and was rewarded for his efforts with an entire room done up in drab gray-green. The whole place resembled some sort of surplus Army vehicle left over from World War II. The bare drywall, in fact, had more character than this color did. Where did he go wrong? By choosing a color at random. This is a sort of roulette that no homeowner can win.

To begin making progress toward a more successful color scheme, start by putting the paint chips away for a moment, and focus on something in your home that you like, in terms of its color. This is how professional decorators will begin. They will pick an object that they know you love, whether it is an oriental rug you brought home from a trip abroad, a certain fabric on a favorite sitting chair, or maybe even an antique vase passed down through the generations. More than just having sentimental value, these objects will then form the beginnings of a color scheme.

A Colorful Inspiration

If you don't happen to have an object that contains colors that can guide your choices for decorating a room, create one. It could be a family heirloom chair in the attic that needs recovering, or an old couch or chair that you've always loved that needs updating. If it's a good-quality piece of furniture, spend the time and money to fix it up, and choose an interesting fabric that can then become the basis for a color scheme.

Faux Finishes Without *Faux* Pas

One of the more interesting ways to change the look of a room is with a *faux* finish. For anyone unschooled in French, this is a fancy way of saying "sponge painting," and involves daubing one or more colors of paint on top of a base coat. Done correctly, *faux* finishing creates a texture and a depth of color that becomes a focal point of a room. There are, of course, a few caveats.

Whether the technique is to add stripes or layers of color, I've found that what works best in *faux* finishing is to choose colors from the same palette. You vary the shades, not the colors. Many times, people try to add drama to *faux* finishes by using contrasting and even clashing colors—navy blue on top of canary yellow, for instance. Don't laugh; I've seen it, and it just doesn't look right. Sticking with the similar colors, especially neutrals or earth-tones, can create a far more natural and appealing effect.

Since there's no single technique that works for everyone, this is a craft that cries out for experimentation. The top coat of paint can be applied with synthetic sheepskin pads, sponges, rollers, and even rags. One *faux* finishing expert I know gets amazing results by using plastic bags from the grocery store. You can pay someone thousands of dollars to create a *faux* finish in a room, or you can have a good deal more fun by learning to do it yourself.

The key, if you take the do-it-yourself route, is to practice. Get a piece of drywall or work inside a closet to make sure you get your technique down. By doing this, you can be assured that you'll end up with a consistent finish or color throughout the room.

Whether you know it or not, you like them because of the colors; this is the psychology of home decorating.

A good decorator will then take a close look at the object, and see what colors can be found in it. It could be a few shades of one color, or an interesting collision of colors. These then become the foundation on which to build a color scheme. The point is that the item you focus on does not have to be large. In some cases it's no more than the swirled base of a pottery lamp, or even the brilliant colors of a pet canary. Working with color charts, wallpaper prints, and swatches of fabric as well as carpeting, designers then work their magic to create an entire chorus of color and texture that harmonize within a room. The result is a complexity of design that you could never achieve just by choosing a paint color for a wall, and then figuring out what else might match it.

While skeptical of this approach at first—which is putting it mildly—I did have the benefit of seeing it put to use in my own house firsthand, and know that it works. My wife and I had a pair of antique chairs that were given to us some years ago, and we had them refinished in a straw-colored paisley fabric. As time went on, the color and the texture grew on us, and they became our favorite objects. Beginning here, the decorator we worked with found a matching straw-yellow color for the walls, which is warm looking and far more daring than we would have chosen on our own. The chair covers also had small streaks of red in them, and we ultimately covered the couches in a red fabric of the same shade. Layer upon layer of choices were made based on what matched and what complemented the fabric in the chairs, and the process seemed to take on a life of its own. Now that the room is finished, the two chairs that started everything have been relegated to a side wall to become accent pieces in the room. Little does anyone know they were actually the source of inspiration for the entire space.

What's with the Windows?

Nothing makes a room feel more alive and even inspirational than natural light. The more light you have, the more vibrant things indoors will be. If you're not sure about whether to add another window or not, go ahead and do it—it's probably the most inexpensive thing you can do to drastically alter the look of a room. But once you have all these windows in place, what do you do with them?

Decorate with restraint, is my advice. Covering everything up with heavy drapes and curtains runs counter to the benefits that windows can bring. Use these window treatments sparingly, so that you don't darken up the room. When it comes to shading out the sun or when you want privacy, there are a few good options that include vertical blinds, horizontal blinds, and, my favorite, plantation shutters. These have all come down remarkably in price, and there are many top-quality manufacturers producing each of them. Plantation shutters, which are installed on the inside of a window rather than the outside, were once considered luxury items that had to be specially ordered. It's gotten to the point now where you can order them and have them custom-cut and ready for installation in about three days. Blinds, too, have come a long way in recent years. While mini-blinds were all the rage in the 1980s and 90s, they've gone the way of "power ties" and padded shoulders in terms of making a fashion statement. A better-looking choice, in my opinion, are blinds that are an inch to an inch

and a half wide. These have less of an institutional look, and can really change the look of your home.

Draperies and other window treatments can look good, too, of course—and the choices of colors and patterns could be the subject of a book all its own. One thing that is important with fabric is to look beyond the color alone and focus on the texture as well. This can add an important dimension to a room's décor. Some of the most popular fabrics in recent years are those that contain what are called microfibers. Visually, these look alive. The synthetic fibers that run through them give the fabric the look of crushed velour, much like Ricardo Montalban had in his Chrysler Cordoba back in the '70s. Don't laugh; it looks great. The fabric can also be embossed with various patterns, which make the color seem more vibrant. Better still is how these fabrics hold up to day-to-day use. They're 100 percent washable, which is something you can't say about the average imported Belgian wool knit. If something spills on it—like your son's or daughter's entire platter of cookies and milk—you can literally wipe the mess away because it will not cling or absorb into the fabric. If you could create a family-friendly fabric just by wishing for it, this would be it.

While we're at it, I would like to sing the praises of valances. These, of course, are those short draperies that hang across the top of the window, rather than extending all the way down to the floor. The beauty of a valance is that it can enhance the look of a window, without limiting the amount of light that comes into a room. At the same time, valances leave most of the window exposed—which is something worth doing, especially if you've spent time trimming the windows in elaborate molding. Why would you want to cover that up with curtains? Because a valance is located high up on the window, it also accomplishes a practical task: It blocks the sunlight during the peak summer hours. This is a distinct advantage, no matter what climate you live in.

Sunblock for Fabrics

Once you've fitted your home with beautiful window treatments and fabric-covered furniture, why watch it all fade in the sun? One smart part of a room makeover involves replacing windows with low-emissivity or "low-e" glass that reduces the damaging ultraviolet rays entering a room. An even more effective solution is heat-mirrored glass, which blocks up to 99 percent of the UV rays.

One thing to consider with draperies, valances, and other window treatments is what sort of material goes on the backside of the fabric—that is, on the side that faces toward the outside of the house. Often these are lined with a plain white fabric, which looks okay from the inside but creates a ghostly presence on the outside. Good interior decorators take a different approach. Instead of using white fabric, they line the valances and draperies with a complementary fabric. That way, when you're outside the house looking in, everything has more of a finished look to it. It's a small detail to consider, to be sure, but a well-appointed house is nothing more than a collection of small details.

Finding the Right Furniture

I have some friends who were so excited about their first home that they rushed to furnish it. Running out to a giant discount furniture store—whose name will be concealed, to protect the guilty—they loaded up on everything from tables and chairs to bookcases and entertainment

The Family Friendly House

With four children under the age of ten, my household is a living laboratory in the family friendly house. Herewith, a few pointers on how to make it all work:

Only use washable paints and wallpapers. For paints, this means either satin eggshell, which has a washable texture, or one of the new washable "flat" paints, of which there are many versions. These aren't perfect, but will keep your home from looking like the hallway at P.S. 11.

Decorate according to what I can best describe as the chronology of your household. In this, I compare it to owning a car. If you have a family, there's definitely a minivan era, where even if you don't own one you can see the advantages. The same is true with décor. Go simple, and with an eye toward what can happen later. I prefer making adjustments in five-year time blocks, which is about when it is time to repaint anyway.

When you can, go for wood trim done in stains or clear finishes rather than paint. Nothing is more durable than stained wood and finished wood. You do it right once, and never have to go back to refinish it. It's the only maintenance-free interior surface I know of.

Choosing the right wall colors can go a long way toward making a house look clean and bright. In short, stay away from light colors, especially white, which will show every mark. While lighter colors do make rooms feel bigger, they'll also make the mess in your home feel bigger. Instead, go for earth tones. These will make rooms feel warmer and are far more forgiving when it comes to keeping the walls clean.

For floors, stick with wood wherever possible. We worry that it scratches, but in fact it's the most forgiving, allows you the most flexibility, and continues to be the only truly renewable surface you can put down. Carpeting can seem appealing—after all, it's so soft—but it comes at a cost. If you can get wall-to-wall carpeting in a household of children to last five years without becoming landfill-worthy, then you will be setting a world record. Instead, go for wood floors, and choose area rugs that can be sent out for cleaning.

An End to Wobbly Joints

When furniture such as a chair starts to wobble, many people try to fix it by squirting a little carpenter's glue along the joint. But this isn't good enough. The key to tightening a joint is to first take it apart. Then, after scraping off any old glue, add new glue to the joint and put the pieces back together. Strap the joints together tightly (an old bicycle inner tube will do), and stay off it for 24 hours. That should fix things. As an alternate, try a product called WonderLok 'Em. Since this flows into the joints more easily than carpenter's glue, you don't necessarily have to remove the pieces first. It dries quickly, in about 30 minutes.

centers they could assemble themselves. They even bought furniture for a home office, and everything cost about half what it might at an authentic furniture store. There was one problem. Everything looked OK, until you touched it. Then when you did, it all seemed as wobbly and stapled together as a cardboard box. I wasn't the only one who felt this way. Within a few months, they realized their mistake, and went about replacing everything with real furniture. In short, they ended up buying everything twice.

Choosing furniture that is made well is every bit as important as choosing furniture that helps create the look you're trying to achieve. But how do you know what's good? You can shop by major brands, such as Thomasville, Henredon, and Baker. But a better approach is to look for solid construction. To begin, ask the salesperson to turn whatever it is you're considering upside down, and then take a close look at it. A quality piece of furniture can be handed down to your family for generations if it's built correctly, and you'll find what you're looking for here. Check for joints that are either finger jointed or doweled and glued together at multiple locations, rather than just stapled together. Look for kiln-dried woods such as hemlock or oak, maple or even birch, as a further sign of quality. Good furniture, like good kitchen cabinets, should be designed to stand up to abuse. Think of Pop in *Hop on Pop,* collapsing into his chair at the end of the day. That's how we use furniture, and that's the sort of stress you want it designed to withstand. If a piece of furniture has drawers in it, open and close them

Rooms to Live In

When it comes to your home, I'm a big believer in furnishing things to your taste, rather than trying to do what's expected. Open up any magazine and you'll see pristine living rooms, devoid of any children's toys or even TV sets and CD players. While this sort of approach might look good, it's not very comfortable to live with.

Instead, I'm an advocate of making the choices that work based on your particular household. If you want to keep the TV out of the living room, that's fine, but there are still ways to make it comfortable, so that you can lounge there on a Sunday afternoon to read the paper, or you can host some impromptu get-togethers with friends and neighbors and their children whenever you like. This can be done by choosing the furniture and materials that hold up to abuse, rather than collapse under it. If you don't have a living room couch that can withstand a few drops of grape juice and cookie crumbs now and then, you've bought the wrong couch.

This goes for the formal dining room, too. If you entertain regularly and will use it, that's great. But if you don't, consider some alternatives; space is too valuable in a home to waste anything. My friends Mike and Judy came up with a clever approach to their dining room. Instead of a formal table, they have a pool table. And on top of it, they have a ping pong table that pieces together. Most of the time, the room is the game room. But when company arrives, they sit at what I like to call "The Fancy Eating Table," as in *The Beverly Hillbillies.* A tablecloth goes over the top, to create the illusion of domestic perfection. With the candles lit, and the food served, no one would ever know what lies underneath—until after dessert when the dishes are cleared, and the real fun begins.

United Colors

Not that I'm an interior decorator, by any means, but I've noticed something odd about many houses that I see. They suffer from jarring color contrasts as you walk through them, with a Red Room here, and a Blue Room there, as if these were some miniature versions of the White House.

Instead, I think houses benefit from being finished in colors and materials that tie together from room to room. The walls vary in slight shades from room to room, in which paints and colors blend into each other, instead of having stark contrasts. I'm not saying you shouldn't do that deep blue dining room. After all, I did in my own home. Just don't go wild with every room in a different color of the rainbow. You'll end up with a kaleidoscope that will give you—and certainly your guests—a headache just walking through it.

again and again, so much that you all but make a nuisance of yourself. This will help convince you that the hardware will function as well in a decade as it does today. If it's cheap construction, you'll know it the instant you feel it.

This may seem like overkill, but the effort will be worth it. When we were first married, my wife and I went shopping for kitchen chairs, and found some that we like. They were expensive, but the store salesman explained that was because they were well constructed. He flipped the chair over, and showed us where the joints had been doweled rather than screwed together. And then he did something remarkable: With the chair tilted over upside down, he jumped up on top of it and stood there, like he had just made an ascent up Mt. Everest. "See?" he said, hopping up and down. "This chair is going to stay together no matter what you do to it, because of the way it's made." He was right. We used the chairs in the kitchen for years, and now use them in our children's arts and crafts area, where they get heavy use. Not one of them wobbles.

Paint and Paper

With a color scheme picked out, it's time to get busy and get to work. I'm a fan of painting, and can tell you that 90 percent of a good paint job is in the prep work, and another 9 percent lies in the choice of the paint itself, particularly in the paint's sheen level.

I've long avoided paints with a flat finish for use on walls, because they are not scrubbable and really don't hold up that well. Try to clean a crayon drawing off the newly painted living room wall, for instance, and you'll end up with an indelible smudge. For this reason, I've always tended to prefer paints that have a satin or eggshell finish, which has only a slight sheen to it but is truly cleanable. Now, however, there is an assortment of new paints produced by nearly every manufacturer that offer washable surfaces in a flat or near-flat sheen. Some actually have a satin or eggshell finish that masquerades as a flat finish; this is technically called "matte." My favorite new paint, however, is a brand by Ace called Sensations that contains Scotchgard as an ingredient, which does not allow dirt and grime to stick at all. I tested a surface coated in this paint myself. After marking it with lipstick and splattering it with grease, I can attest that it washed right off with an ordinary cleaner. It even cleaned up better than a semi-gloss paint.

Wallpaper, for me, is another matter. Here, moderation counts for every-

How to Wash a Wall

There are many multipurpose cleaners that are specially designed to wash walls, and all do a fairly good job. What I've found that works the best, however—and also costs the least—is ordinary dish soap, warm water, and a sponge. Keep in mind that if you're too aggressive with your sponging, or if you use a sponge with an abrasive pad, you will remove the paint. Give the solution a chance to soak in and you'll have an easier time of removing any marks or stains on the walls, no matter what the paint finish.

The Ultimate Fashion Statement

While surveying your house room by room to see what can be changed in terms of décor, don't overlook some essential elements: smoke and carbon monoxide detectors, as well as fire extinguishers.

Smoke detectors are the ones we're most familiar with, and belong on each floor, near the sleeping areas, and near (but not in) the kitchen. Keeping one just outside the kitchen should reduce the sensitivity slightly so that you can burn the odd piece of toast here and there without the detector going off. The exact placement of smoke detectors is subject to local building codes, however—and those will have to be heeded.

Carbon monoxide detectors are very important, for a number of reasons. They are designed to sense the backflow of odorless fumes from a furnace or boiler into a house, which can be potentially lethal and may not necessarily be accompanied by any overt smoke. Carbon monoxide is heavier than air, so it sinks to the floor of a room. For this reason, I would recommend also putting the carbon monoxide detector down closer to the floor, so that it will trigger more quickly and give you time to act. Both smoke detectors and carbon monoxide detectors have a definite life span, and last an average of about ten years. If you're not sure how old a unit

thing, since it involves patterns and designs that can easily overwhelm a room and even an entire house. The trick to choosing a paper or style is to go for subtlety. In my own house, I have one room, the powder room, that is wallpapered. It wouldn't matter if we had the loudest wallpaper on the planet; the fact that it is contained inside that one little room makes it palatable. I also have wallpapering in the kitchen, but in two specific areas—a wall with a chair rail, that has complementary stripes and floral design above and below, and another small area that has a third matching striped pattern. Where wallpaper can get away from you is if you try to use it to decorate an entire living room or family room or hallway that runs upstairs. Even the simplest design can sudis, err on the side of caution and replace it. The benefit of what they do compared to what they cost is more than worth the added expense.

A fire extinguisher in an easy-to-reach location is also essential, especially in a kitchen. You should also keep an extra one in the main coat closet in the hall, especially if you have a fireplace in the nearby living room. Simply buying a fire extinguisher isn't enough, however. Make sure you read the instructions, and keep a watch on the expiration date to ensure yours is in tip-top condition at all times. Lastly, remember this rule of thumb: If a fire is larger than a wastepaper basket, don't risk trying to fight it yourself. Get out of the house, and dial 911.

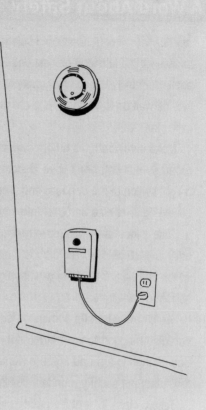

denly turn into an overpowering visual assault, in my opinion, similar to what happens when you've been dozing in a darkened room and someone steps in and abruptly switches on the lights. You blink, you shake your head, you feel disoriented. This, at its worst, is what too much wallpaper can do. Use it sparingly, or don't use it at all.

Most of my experience with wallpaper has been removing it, rather than installing it, and this deserves some special mention. Nothing slows up a renovation process more than having an entire room—or in some cases, an entire house—that has been gummed with layer upon layer of wallpaper. Fortunately, technology has kept pace with the task. It used to be that your only option was to score the walls with a

the cloth at one edge and the paper peels away with it. Since you're not saturating the wall to the extent that you would by the other methods, there's little risk of damaging drywall beneath it. A $20 package might be enough to do a 10-foot section of wall, and will save you hundreds of dollars in aggravation.

With the rooms properly decorated, let's turn now to ways to keep it looking good, by managing all the clutter that the typical household produces.

chapter FOUR

Aflutter over Clutter
The need to find storage space can lead to creative—and often attractive—solutions.

My friends Minnie and Hector have a great-looking house. It's not grand; it's not lavish. What it is, is neat—in a way that works for them.

They've got three children, but instead of chaos there's a quiet sense of organization to the family. The boots and shoes go into closet dividers that are under a bench near the front door. The clothes and jackets and mittens go into a drawer, or clipped to a drying rack if they're wet. In the living room, there's a computer table for the kids, complete with a built-in shelf for all the video games and CD-ROMS, and even a place for all the videos and DVDs by the television. If you show up unexpectedly they'll apologize for the place being a mess, as would anyone else, but it's really nothing of the sort. It's tidy and comfortable, and even the way things are stored has a stylish flair. You open the closet, filled with tennis rackets and ski equipment and horse-riding helmets and boots, and even this looks well ordered. What's best is that the children know the routine, not because they're bullied and browbeaten, but because if you have a logical place to put things, you tend to put them away automatically. When cleanup time comes, there's a place for everything.

Helping Kids Get Organized

Back in the 1960s, Dustin Hoffman was given some very good advice in *The Graduate* about the future of society: "Plastics," he was told. Everyone scoffed then, but how true this has turned out, as anyone who has seen the Lego- or doll-littered floor of the average ten-year-old's-room can attest. Fortunately, there is a great solution for all of this stuff, and it, too, is plastic.

While I love plastic totes and boxes for my own storage, they also work well for children's toys. The beauty of these for kids is that they can grab a box, dump it on the ground, and get playing. The beauty for parents is that these make an easy storage method that kids will actually like using. In my own household, we put a bunch of these cabinets in the basement playroom along with some wicker baskets that fit neatly on the shelves. Each has become a storage container for certain items—such as one for toy instruments, another for anything with wheels, and another for anything with arms and legs and heads, no matter in what proportion.

It's hardly the Dewey Decimal System, to be sure, but it does help keep things loosely organized. And it's a system that children like and are actually able to maintain themselves—which is the most beautiful thing of all.

So much of our home renovation attempts focus on the way things look. But the foundation for this is an organizational system that works. You could have the most luxurious taste and a budget large enough to bring it into reality, but what would be the point if your home is lost in a sea of stuff? Tame this mess, however, and it won't matter how lavish your room is; your home will be warm and inviting, like Hector and Minnie's place. True, neatness doesn't rank as an architectural style, the way Art Deco or Early Federal does, but it's every bit as beautiful to look at. When it's absent, the result is a house heaped with possessions. In a jumbled place like this, homeowners are condemned to having to shuffle things around from the attic, to the basement, to the garage, as well as from room to room, in the desperate hope to make use of every available inch of space. It becomes a real-life version of one of those little puzzles, where you have to slide the squares around incessantly from corner to corner in an attempt to create a clear picture.

Believe me, there's a better way. Let's take a look at the possibilities, from managing the mess to finding creative and attractive ways to store it all.

Start at the Beginning

Home organization has become all but an obsession, judging by the amount of information that's available on it and the number of professional "home organizers" who will be more than willing to come in and do the task for a fee. The only solution that will work, however, is one that you have created yourself—and adapted to the way you live. It will be helpful, however, to focus on what these professionals do. In essence, they zero in on two things: What have you got? And what space have you got to store it in? While this may sound simple, it is the key to understanding how to solve and manage your storage problems.

Let's begin with the first step, which is to assess what it is you actually own. For many people, including myself, this is not an easy question at all. Too often, every square foot of a house is filled, including closets, cabinets, basements, attics, garages, and even sheds. It's time to act like a business manager at a warehouse, and take an inventory.

Literally start from one end of the house and go to the other, and make a list in every room of items that need to be stored, from clothes in the closets to camping equipment in the basement. The act of making this list alone will create a shock, especially as you unearth things that haven't been used in years, such as the entire oeuvre of *Mad* magazine, or perhaps a box containing an inventory of prom dresses. With the same thrill of the archaeologists discovering the remains of Troy,

Adding a Closet

Does your home have a shortage of closet space? If the answer is yes, hold a yard sale or make a few trips to the local thrift shop. If the answer is still yes, it may be time to add a closet or two. In most cases, even in homes with a pinched floor plan, it is usually possible to eke out enough room for a decent-sized storage area.

To begin, take a look at the rooms in your home and see if any are shaped irregularly. Many older homes in particular have small nooks, where they abut bathrooms or kitchens. If this is the case, your task is easy: That nook can be framed into a closet, and still leave you with a logically shaped room—albeit, a slightly smaller one. A reduced floor area, however, is a small price to pay for extra closet space.

If you have two smaller rooms that can't accommodate a closet, the solution may lie in enlarging one of the rooms and creating a storage area out of the left-over space. In many cases the divider between two small rooms may be a simple partition wall. This has nothing to do with the structure of your house, and can easily be moved. Other times, the partition is a load-bearing wall, which literally carries the weight of the house above. This can still be moved, but will require an additional beam added to support the house. A good contractor will know exactly how to do it.

Ideally, a closet should be 26 inches deep, but it can also be far less, especially if the goal is to create shelves rather than hanging rods for clothes.

you will no doubt find things that haven't seen the light of day since you moved into your house. Target these for the giveaway pile, and keep your sentimentality in check.

When you've made a list of what you own, start organizing according to where things need to be stored. That pile of videos and DVDs, for instance, should be kept near the television. That collection of Elton John record albums from the 1970s should be near the turntable—and if you don't actually have a turntable or have any intention of ever playing a record again, this is as good a time as any to ax the collection for good. Basements make great storage for children's toys and sports equipment. If you're not lucky enough to have a basement, look to the attic or even an area in the garage for these things.

The Two-Year Test

In organizing things in your home, try putting things through a simple challenge: Have you used them in the last two years? If yes, hold onto them. If no, then target them for donation or pass them along to friends or family. You probably won't miss the things at all.

Getting organized in this way not only helps you find all your stuff, it's good for you psychologically. It reduces stress in the long run, and more than makes up for the momentary anxiety of having to part with something.

Building the Space You Need

One of my favorite additions to a room is a built-in storage area, which is the perfect combination of form and function. Who doesn't love the look of a well-crafted bookcase in a classic living room, or a window seat that lifts up to reveal a storage chest for spare blankets and pillows? These are elegant ways to solve the storage problem, and they can add real value to your home, as well. Show me a home with well-planned built-ins, and I'll show you a home that will have prospective buyers

Keep It Flexible

When adding built-ins, the goal is to keep them as flexible as possible in terms of storage. To do this, always have them installed with adjustable shelves. This way, the space intended for holding knickknacks today can be adjusted to hold large books tomorrow.

falling over themselves to make an offer for it the moment it goes on the market.

Built-ins require great care, however, beginning with their location. The funny thing about built-ins, to me, is that they will almost tell you where they should be located, based on the layout of a room. Now, I am not pretending to be "The Furniture Whisperer," or anything like this, but the locations for these become fairly obvious as you live in a house. It could be one end of the living room, or an alcove at the top of a staircase, or a space beneath a dormered window in a bedroom. Sometimes, built-ins can be added to help better define a space. A peninsula, for instance, can be a built in such a way that it goes along a wall, and then curves out to divide a room into two separate areas. No matter how it is set up, a built-in also gives you the benefit of added storage space.

Whenever you're considering built-ins, your goal should be to reinforce certain design elements in a room, not just shoehorn them in wherever they might fit. You want the built-in to look as if it was built in with the house, not added years later. Built-ins can be custom-made, which is the most expensive way to go. Or they can be created from stock cabinets and ready-made detail pieces. These, combined with a little bit of creative carpentry, can result in a look that's every inch as good as custom, yet far less expensive. Let's talk first about custom cabinets.

The beauty of having built-ins custom-made is that they can exactly match any piece of detailing in a home. The bookcases and base cabinets that I had built in my living room, for instance, were installed by my friend, Simon, who is a cabinetmaker. I wanted there to be some way to tie them in to the rest of the room. To do this, I matched the baseboard trim in the room, and wrapped it around the new units. I didn't take the cabinets all the way to the ceiling, however, because the ornate crown molding would have been too difficult to match. Instead, I kept the bookcases down about six inches from the ceiling, exactly even with a picture rail that ran around the top of the walls. This was easier to match, so I topped the bookcases with a similar molding, which helped tie things together.

Taking things a step further, Simon noticed a small ornate design in the center of the original fireplace mantel. He was able to duplicate this design by hand-carving it into the edge of the base cabinets. It's not an exact replica, to be sure, but it's in the same style. Since we moved in, I have had countless people tell me how much they like the room. "It just love the way they used to match mantels and bookcases in old houses," one guest recently told me. I agreed—leaving him none the wiser.

Now, in addition to custom furniture, stock cabinetry also offers tremendous possibilities for built-ins. People somehow think this

How to Find a Stud

When you're securing a built-in to a wall, you sure don't want to have to guess where the stud is located. Instead, spend $10 to buy an electronic stud finder. This simple device beeps or flashes a light when passed over a stud and makes the task easy.

belongs only in the kitchen. In addition to the ready-made cabinets that are available, most good cabinet manufacturers also offer stock detailing, such as moldings and trim, that can be used to create a built-in look anywhere in the house. With a little bit of carpentry and some ingenuity, stock parts can come together to create a custom look.

One thing is important whether the cabinet is custom or stock, and that is to carefully design the area where it meets the floor. In the kitchen, cabinets are fitted with what is called a toe kick, which is a recessed area that allows you to stand close to the countertop without banging your toes into the cabinet. That's fine while you're chopping vegetables and washing dishes, but you won't need that anywhere else in the house. In fact, a toe kick on anything will look like it belongs in the kitchen, no matter where it's installed.

You can order most kitchen cabinets without toe kicks, but the problem is that they will then be too low to the ground. The result will be awkward looking. One way around this is to build a raised platform a few inches high for the cabinets to rest on. The platform is then

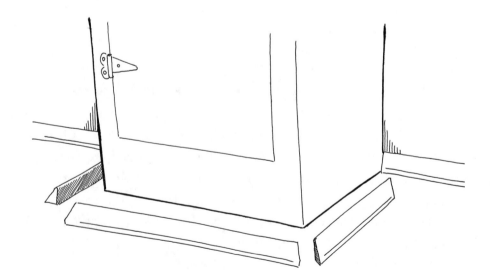

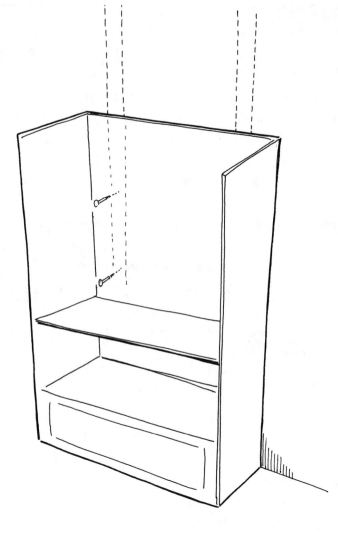

trimmed with the same baseboard molding used in the rest of the room, to create a seamless look. Whether it's painted or stained, this portion of the trim should be finished off exactly like the trim in the rest of the room. Up toward the ceiling, you can create a similar put-together look by wrapping the crown molding against the front of a cabinet or bookcase, if it extends that high.

Get Packing

Everyone has a unique solution for creating an organized home. For me, it comes down to one thing: Learn how to pack efficiently.

While I am terrible at clearing things out and parting with items I no longer use (which is why I have a closet full of Chicago Cubs caps), I make up for this by organizing things extremely well. If we're going on a trip as a family and I've got to pack the car, show me what needs to be taken and I'll get it in there—right down to the dog crate. I think that same philosophy works in organizing all the things you need and use inside your home, as well.

The way to do this is to find out exactly what you have, then start putting the puzzle together. It's like building a house. You don't just work on one little area like the kitchen, then remember that you have the entire rest of the house to factor in. Instead, you start with the big picture, then use that to guide you through the details. If you've got things in closets, things in the attic, things in the basement, and other things scattered all over the house, take an inventory of everything rather than working room by room.

One thing that is important is to securely attach bookcases to the wall. With anything over 5 feet tall, there's a risk that it could tip over as it becomes loaded up. To prevent this, the built-in needs to be secured with a 3-inch wood screw drilled directly into the framing of the wall—not just into the drywall or plaster. This means that the screw has to penetrate into the structural board called the stud that runs vertically in the wall. Every tall built-in, I believe, should be secured with at least two screws. If you're having an extensive number of built-ins installed, the best approach is to add small bits of lumber known as blocking into the wall itself between the studs. This allows more screws to be used to provide an even stronger connection to the wall.

To tame this mess, I am a huge believer in the plastic tote or storage box because it literally creates a building block for your organizational system. Take a look around in your basement, for instance and you'll find lots of items that would never stack up or even stay on a shelf, such as old toys, spare light bulbs, an assortment of paint brushes and rollers. Tuck them in a plastic box, and suddenly you're dealing with things that are stackable as well as sealable. While boxes come in just about every color in the plastic rainbow, I'm a fan of ones that are clear or transluscent, so you can figure out what's inside without having to open them up. This makes those Halloween costumes or holiday decorations easy to find when you need them.

One warning about stock cabinets: Many times, even good-quality cabinets have a flimsy plywood backing. This is more for decoration than for structure, and will hardly keep a built-in from tipping no matter how many screws you use; in the event of a mishap, the whole back will simply rip off. In these cases, it's important to add additional framing, such as an inconspicuous board that connects two sides of a bookcase, to the furniture itself, so that it can be then be secured to the wall in a permanent way.

A Clothes Call

Let me start by making a bold statement: I believe that whoever invented the "rod and shelf" configuration found in most closets should be prosecuted and sentenced to a life of hard labor. For instance, how about folding and cramming everything into a closet day after day, until the error of the design becomes self-evident?

A configuration that involves a single rod with a shelf above it is the worst possible design for maximizing space that anyone could ever have dreamed up. It might have worked back in the 1920s, when the average wardrobe for both men and women consisted of a dress suit

Passing the Clothes

While I have not conducted a scientific survey, I am willing to bet what the number one form of clutter is—at least in families with children. Toys, perhaps, but more than this it's clothes that no longer fit. While it's easy to get rid of clothes that are worn out, nothing is more painful than giving away a $50 winter jacket or $20 pair of jeans that were outgrown in half a season. These languish in drawers and closets, because who wants to give them all away?

One thing that works in my family—and would also work in yours, either with relatives or a close set of friends—is to create a system in which these clothes are passed back and forth as they are needed. It's one thing to pass along an item or two; in my family, we pass along the whole wardrobe. Between my family and all of my wife's siblings, there are at least a dozen children, with more every moment it seems. As a rule, we take the outgrown clothes, and group them according to gender and size. There might be a boys' tub for ages five to seven, and a girls' tub for ages ten to twelve. Then, when we have a get-together, we end up swapping tubs, usually in the driveway back and forth from one minivan to another.

As the clothes are passed along, the contents change as old things are whittled down and new things added. But keeping them in constant motion, like a juggling act, prevents them from resting too long in any one family's closet.

or two, a couple of hats, and a couple of pairs of shoes. But for the way we live today, it is the worst use of space imaginable. Of all the homeowners I've met through the years, I've never heard anyone say, "I have too many closets." There are some ways to increase your closet efficiency, however, which are a lot simpler than building new closets.

The approach is to think of a closet as a mini-room, not just some hole in the wall in which to stuff and hang things at random. It's a mini-room that needs to be thought out in terms of design, in the same way you think about the layout in your living room or kitchen. You can have elaborate walk-in closets or tiny ones that hold only a few coats. No matter what the particulars, you will be amazed at the difference that proper organization can yield. Suddenly, that closet that held very little now brims with everything from clothes, boots, shoes, umbrellas, gloves, hats, and everything else that follows us along in our daily lives. Better yet, everything is easy to access. Let's go over some of the basics.

Hang It Up

What's one of the best upgrades you can make for a closet? Good hangers. Fill your closet with the metal hangers that come free from the dry cleaners, and you're asking for trouble. Not only are they hard to handle, but they leave two little points in shirts and blouses and jackets hung on them from the metal tips. Wear these clothes, and you look like you have a couple of antennae coming out of your shoulders. Instead, spring for larger hangers made of plastic or wood that have a wider profile, about an inch or so. Your clothes will thank you.

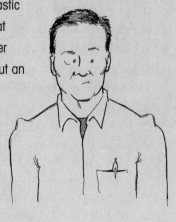

Reclaiming the Garage

While we're on the subject of clutter, I would like to point out what is most likely the most cluttered spot in your home: The garage. We tend to jam everything in the garage; I certainly do. If you take a tour there, you'll find the lawn-mower, four kids' bicycles, two wagons, two strollers, garden tools, and enough basketballs to host a training camp for the Chicago Bulls. What you won't find in there, oddly, are my two cars, because they simply don't fit.

The solution for a messy garage is the same as for any other area of your house. Namely, purge, reorganize, and purge again. When you've gotten rid of the detritus, including that pile of forty-year-old *Life* magazines and the box of parts to a car you sold a decade ago, it's time to create a storage system. The easiest approach is to line the walls with industrial-strength wire shelving, which will hold up to the rigors of garage life far better than wooden or plastic shelves. Next, buy a set of plastic storage boxes, and group everything by category. You could have one box for car-washing equipment, one for the lawn games, and another for all those bungee cords.

Don't forget about ceiling hooks, either. They're great for getting little-used items like extension ladders up and out of the way. Keep at this for a weekend or two and, who knows, you might even be able to fit your car in there.

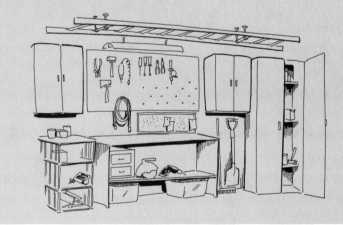

With a closet, everyone who has spent any time at all organizing these spaces eventually comes up with a configuration that works for them. I'd like to describe some of the dimensions that work for me. Let's start with a rod for hanging clothes—which is fine, as long as it's not the only thing you add to a closet. The best height for a single rod setup is between 66 and 72 inches, which is the easiest height to reach when you open the closet door. Rather than a single-rod closet, however, I prefer adding a second rod in some cases, which doubles the volume of hanging space. True, you can't hang long coats and gowns or trousers in this space, but you can reserve a portion of the closet for these, and use double rods for the rest. A second rod needs to be no closer to the floor than 42 inches, which will allow you enough space to hang coats and jackets, shirts and pants that are folded on a hanger. In this case, the top rod needs to be 42 inches above this one, which positions it at 84 inches, or 7 feet. It may be slightly higher than is comfortable to reach, but it will be useful for holding seasonal clothes or clothes worn less frequently. One caution: If a rod extends more than 4 feet, as it would in a double closet, it will need to be supported by a bracket in the center so that it does not buckle under the weight of all those clothes.

In addition to rods, adding shelves to an existing closet is a great way to add additional space. For shelving, there are a few options. The simplest is the myriad of closet kits available that are easy to install, such as the ELFA system available at the Container Store, or an assortment of components available through Closet Maid. What makes these systems work well is that they have predrilled holes and are easy to install. You could literally install them in an afternoon. Once in place, the systems can be customized by adding rod systems, basket systems, shelving, and an assortment of other components. These come in infinite configurations that you can put together yourself, as well as an endless number of color variations, including white, black, and chrome. Working this way, you can increase your storage capacity over the old rod-and-shelf configuration by 30 to 60 percent in an afternoon—and the best part is the price. It might cost about $500 to reconfigure a large bedroom closet. Compare this to the $2,500 cost of having a professional come in and do the same thing. An additional advantage to the wire shelves is that they don't collect dust in the same way that wooden shelves do—all you need to do is wipe them down once a year with a damp cloth, and your maintenance is done.

In Defense of the Shed

In our current age of way too much stuff, I think a shed can provide a truly useful solution to some of the clutter. It can free up the garage by becoming a place to store the yard tools, the lawnmower, and even the jars, cans, and newspapers destined for recycling.

A shed does not have to be ugly. When I was growing up, my father built one in the backyard that looked like a miniature version of our house. It had the same siding, a beautiful entry door in the center, and two little windows on the side complete with flower boxes. Along the side, he built a dog run, with a doggiedoor that led inside. Inside, he added a workbench, and stored things such as the lawnmower. He even had a cage with rabbits. While the shed wasn't much bigger than 8 feet by 8 feet, it ended up being packed with a lot of fond memories of the time I spent there with him.

You can build a noble shed yourself, or have someone do it for you. At a trade show, I discovered handsome sheds built by Amish carpenters that can be trucked around the country. These are the antithesis of the modern metal shed, and are more like fine carpentry because of the workmanship and craftsmanship. They mimic the look of old red barns with their tongue-and-groove construction and classic rooflines. These also have wood floors, which I think makes a great deal of sense compared to one that has no floor at all, especially when it rains.

A Painted Surface to Live With

Since a closet is a mini-room, it has to be painted on the inside. But instead of choosing flat or low-sheen paints as you might in other rooms, use satin-eggshell or semi-gloss enamel on the wall. In addition to being easy to keep clean, these paints hold up better to the rigors of being in a closet.

As convenient as they are and easy to install, these wire systems sometimes lack the substantial feel that wood shelves have. You can hire someone to install furniture-quality shelves, of course, but this seems to run counter to the spirit of what a closet is: It's a room with the door closed most of the time. I don't know how much anyone would want to invest in a closet by putting mahogany or teak or oak in there; to me certainly a painted finish in a closet is perfectly adequate. As far as materials, I'm all for utility. What works best for shelving, I have found, is ¾-inch medium density fiberboard, or MDF, which is as inexpensive as it is sturdy. This is sold either in large dimensions, or in precut shelving that has a rounded bullnose edge. In addition to low cost, this material has two good qualities. Shelves made from it paint easily, and they turn out to be very strong.

Unlike the wire shelf systems that go in quickly, wooden shelves take time to install. The shelves will need to be supported with what are called cleats around the perimeter, which are boards about 1 inch thick and 2 inches wide. These provide a solid support for the shelves to rest on. The cleats have to be attached to structural boards in the wall with 3-inch wood screws, rather than nails, since nails have a bad habit of prying loose over time. Strong as MDF is, if a shelf made from it has to span a distance greater than 30 inches, it will need to be supported in the center. Here, there are two options. One is to add an angle bracket that is attached with screws to the wall beneath the shelf. The other is to add a center support cleat, which is literally a post that runs from the floor to the ceiling and helps carry the load. Without either of these, wide shelves will bow and could eventually buckle.

Now that everything is in its proper place, let's have a little fun and turn to some electrical gadgets that can bring some high-wattage enjoyment to your household.

chapter FIVE

Electrifying Decisions
These electrical upgrades can make your home both safer—and a whole lot more fun—to live in.

A few years ago, I was invited to tour "The House of the New Millennium," and have yet to recover. At a quick glance, the house looked like any other well-built home, with thick wood trim, beautiful tray ceilings, and lavish décor. It looked like it was something out of the pages of *Architectural Digest*. In the realm of electronics, however, it more resembled something out of *Battlestar Galactica*.

To call the home cutting edge would be an understatement. The whole place was controlled by touch screens placed in every room, which were used to monitor every aspect of life indoors. Heating and air conditioning could be adjusted in individual rooms, to an absurd degree. One bedroom, for instance, could be kept at a perfect 72 degrees in the winter, while the one next to it could be chilled slightly to 71. Video monitors positioned everywhere made it possible to keep tabs on whoever was home, whether it was the kids hanging out in the basement playroom or a baby taking a nap upstairs. The home electronics system tapped into the power of the Internet, which made it possible to control every single aspect of it from afar. When the doorbell rang, for instance, it was possible for the homeowner to log onto a laptop computer to see who was there, then unlock the door for them by remote control to let whoever it was inside—even if the homeowner happened to be lying on the beach in Barbados at the time.

Like it or not, this is where technology is headed. Before the decade is out, homes will be rigged with wireless technology that creates seamless connections between us and our gadgets. While I'm not advocating that everyone rush out and create homes worthy of George Jetson, I am going to make a case for a few tried-and-true electrical devices that can actually make a difference in your home. Rather than being fads, these are appliances and systems that have been proven to work and, what's more, have been proven to be durable and add real value to a home.

Let's take a look at some electrical conveniences, as well as some devices that will make your home safer.

A Theater at Home

I toured a house once that contained a media room that would rival anything in a movie theater; it looked as if it had been built by a modern-day William Randolph Hearst. Located in a windowless lower level, the cavernous room sloped down toward the screen, and was filled with tiers of leather couches set in a half circle. As you watched, the sound was so realistic that it felt as if you were inside Nicole Kidman's head while she spoke. Astounding, to be sure, but what was even more mind-boggling was the price tag. The owners paid more than $500,000 for the room and all the equipment—which would sure pay for a lot of popcorn and jujubes at the local octoplex.

Let's face it, we all want a great movie-watching experience at home, but we sure don't want to pay outrageous amounts for it. Show me a person who is happy spending $10,000 on a home theater setup, and I'll show you someone who either has a lot of excess money to throw around or just wants to show off their equipment. Fortunately, there have been huge advances in both sound and movie-playing technology that can allow anyone to turn their home into a home theater, for a fraction of this cost. Granted, this may not be the sort of place where Tom Cruise will

Sounding Off

A home theater can be a great thing—except to anyone in the house who isn't part of the action. All of that sub-woofing and multi-speakered sound can quickly grow annoying. Keeping a lid on the sound is as much an essential ingredient of a home theater as good sound itself. There are a few things that can be done structurally to accomplish this with relative ease.

To create a truly soundproof room requires extraordinary engineering and expense. It's something you'd find only at a lab at MIT, or perhaps a recording studio. Instead, your goal is to minimize the amount of sound that passes from the home theater to the rest of the house. The easiest way to do this is to increase the density of the walls and the ceiling. One way this can be accomplished is by adding more insulation. If you're renovating a room, you can effectively reduce sound transmission just by adding ordinary fiberglass insulation to the ceilings and walls. This will muffle the noise, and take the sharpest jangles out of the noise that passes through to the rest of the house. Using foam insulation will reduce noise transmission even further.

In addition, putting a double layer of drywall on the walls and ceiling can also go a long way toward containing the sound. Here, you want to make sure that you don't align the seams in the two layers of drywall. Instead, the drywall should be installed with no overlapping seams, to create the densest space.

The result will be near-silence, which is the sweetest sound of all.

stage his next movie premiere, but it will more than get the job done well. Let's start with sound.

One of the big trends now is to install a sound system in which music is piped in throughout the home. These systems consist of two major elements in terms of setting them up—namely, the speakers, and the wires that connect them. The key to these systems is that they should be as unobtrusive as possible. You don't want your room to be dominated by a pair of waist-high speakers in the corner, the way you did in your college dorm, nor do you want to navigate a spaghetti-tangle of wires running across the floor. Instead, there are fairly simple ways to make these elements disappear, yet deliver sound with a superb quality.

With speakers, there's a straightforward way to install them seamlessly into a home. Many manufacturers make what are called recessed speakers designed to be inserted right into a wall; you can literally paint

Don't Use a Fuse!

If you're trying to gauge the status of your home's electrical system, there's a simple pass/fail test you can perform, and it goes like this: Does your home have circuit breakers? You pass. Does it have fuses? You fail.

Modern circuit breakers are designed to shut off instantaneously if there's a current overload or a short circuit. No power, no problem. Old-fashioned fuses, however, stop functioning *almost* instantaneously if there's a short circuit, and that's the problem. In that brief time it takes for them to blow, an overheated wire or spark can set fire to the entire house. Many insurance companies flat-out refuse to insure a home that has fuses, and since they're basing this decision on statistics rather than on some whim, I think it's wise to take the hint.

Upgrading the wiring in a home is not difficult, and it certainly is a selling point if you ever choose to put your home on the market. Switching to circuit breakers and making other improvements in the electrical service might cost anywhere from $1,000 to $2,500. It's an essential expenditure to safeguard your home.

A Woofer Worth Barking About

One of the reasons recessed speakers work so well is because they actually use the wall cavity as a sounding board for extra resonance. Even so, no home theater system is complete without a sub-woofer speaker. This gives you a big bass sound—like the thump of the tyrannosaurus in *Jurassic Park.* Rather than being installed in a wall, the sub-woofer has to sit on the floor to create the optimal thumping effect.

over the grills once they're in place so that you don't even notice them. Not only are these practically invisible, but the sound quality they produce is tremendous. While I'm no stereo guru, I do know when Springsteen and Abba sound right. For brands, look for speakers by Bose, Sonance, and Inwall, as well as Eclipse, all of which excel at producing these special speakers.

Mounting them in a wall is easier than it might at first seem. The recessed speakers come with templates, which are literally pieces of paper printed with the size opening that is required to be cut into the wall. With a pencil, you trace around the template onto the wall, then use either a drywall saw or a utility knife to cut the shape. If you've cut it right, the speaker fits right into the circle, and the speaker housing covers the damage from the cut. The beauty of this is that there's no patching to do whatsoever. You pop the speakers in place, and the job is done. These speakers come in both circular and rectangular shapes, and either style can be installed in a wall built with drywall. If you have plaster walls, however, the challenge is greater because the material is harder to cut. You actually have to cut, chisel, and chip the material out, which includes removing the wooden strips called lath behind the plaster. The proper tool for this is a circular saw. Despite its name, you can't cut circles with a circular saw. For this reason, you should search for rectangular speakers if you're installing them in a plaster wall. You'll create a lot of dust during the project, but this is one way to ensure the cleanest cut with minimal damage.

While the speakers are important, the quality of the speaker wire is every bit as essential. Here, thicker is better, since a thicker wire offers less resistance in the signal coming through the wire—in the same way that more water can pour out of a larger garden hose. You'll have to go by the numbers: Choose nothing thinner than 14-gauge stranded copper wire. The lower the number, the thicker the wires. An even better choice would be 12-gauge wire, but they also come in 10-gauge varieties as well. Speaker wire can be inexplicably expensive; some of it sells for hundreds and even thousands of dollars per foot. Unless you're planning to open a recording studio, this is a ludicrous waste of money. In most cases, you'll be able to get away with 14-gauge wire. Now, there are two ways to shop

Is There an Electrician in the House?

Electrical work ranks as one of the most dangerous jobs for a novice to tackle alone. Unless you're willing to get training to do it, I would recommend avoiding it, even for simple jobs, such as installing a light fixture or a switch. Instead, you should call a professional to help. In all cases, look for a licensed electrician, rather than for someone who is practicing without a license.

How can you tell if an electrician is any good or not? One indication: They're notoriously busy. It might be four months before they can work you into their schedule, which is a long time to wait for someone to put a dimmer switch in. When you find one, ask for their license number to make sure they have one, and check to see that it's current. That way, you'll know the person you're hiring is qualified to do the work.

Electricians can be expensive. It might cost $75 to have a single dimmer switch installed. Here's where economies of scale can help, because if it's two dimmer switches, it won't be $150, but it might cost $80. It's a question of how much work is involved, because once the number goes up, the cost per device goes down.

for it. You can buy the speaker wire at a specialty audio store, where you will spend upward of $1 a foot. That may sound cheap, until you start to wire the upstairs and the downstairs and realize that hundreds of feet of wiring are involved. A better choice is to go to an ordinary hardware store and buy a bulk spool of the same gauge wire. You can probably find it for under 25 cents per foot.

If you're adding this wiring to a new house or a new addition, nothing could be easier. The wire runs through the gaps between the bare studs, right to the location of the speakers. If you're adding this to an existing house, however, you've got some additional work to do. Where the recessed speakers are installed in drywall, it's a fairly easy task to run the wires to them. The whole process resembles ice fishing, to a certain extent. You have to drop the wire down into the hole that you've cut for the speakers. Then—while being careful to tie one end of the wire to a large piece of wood so it does not completely disappear into the wall—you have to fish it out from below. In some cases, you can go into the basement and find the wire, which makes the task simple. You then carefully staple the wire to the framing and lead it to the point where the stereo receiver will be located, drill a hole up and into the floor, then poke the wire back up into the room.

If it's not possible to string the wire through the basement, you may

Sound Advice

Once you figure out how to install a pair of recessed speakers, it's possible to install them everywhere in the house—in the bathroom, the kitchen, the screened-in porch, you name it. The problem is that most stereos have a two-channel system, which means they can run a maximum of four speakers. Try to run six or eight of them and the stereo will burn out quickly. To protect against this, make sure you install a device called a protection splitter on the back of the stereo. This heavy-gauge wire contains buttons that allow you to select which speakers you want turned on, and protects your stereo from overloading.

have to be more creative. The most common method in this case is to remove the baseboard trim that runs along the bottom of the wall. The wire is then fished out of the wall from where the cut for the recessed speaker was made, then tucked into the gap behind the trim to run around the perimeter of the room. When it's in place, the trim is nailed back into position and repainted. The same process works for plaster walls, but the risk of blistering the plaster and creating a massive mess is

An Accent on Recessed Lighting

Adding recessed or "can" lighting can make a great improvement to a room—as long as you adhere to a few guidelines. Since these lights are permanent additions, it's important to get them right.

The first step is to choose the right recessed lights, and this will vary according to whether the ceiling is insulated or not. If there is no insulation, ordinary recessed lights will do. If there is insulation, you need to upgrade to a different kind of unit called an IC light, which stands for "insulated can." The danger here is that the insulation in the ceiling can trap the heat emitted by ordinary lights, and create a fire hazard. The IC lights prevent this. While the lights look similar when installed, the housing that holds the IC light is different. It is much larger on the back end, with a metal housing that resembles a breadbox. This is designed to keep a distance between the light and the insulation, and to provide enough of a gap for it to release heat without creating a fire hazard. All local building codes require these to be used in insulated areas for safety, and every licensed electrician knows how to do this. But for people tackling their own electrical work—and many do—using the wrong lights is a common, and very dangerous, mistake.

The second step with recessed lights is to use some restraint in positioning. Too many lights poked into a ceiling can turn it into a surface that resembles Swiss cheese. Be sure to follow the manufacturer's instructions on placement of the lights, which will help rein in the look.

A Warning about Electricity

So many aspects of home renovation look as if they'd be easy to do yourself—from painting, to a little carpentry, to changing faucets. Where you should draw the line is with electricity. Unless you're going to take a serious look at what is safe and what is not, my advice would be to leave this to a professional. What's $50 or even $100 to hire someone to come in and install a light fixture, compared with the potentially disastrous consequences that could result from doing it wrong? It's not worth the risk. Even so, many people insist on tinkering with their electrical systems, and here's where a few essential safety tips can come in handy.

The first is to turn off the power to whatever light fixture or outlet you're working on. This doesn't mean switching the thing off; it means going to the electrical service box and shutting off the circuit breaker that controls that circuit or unscrewing the fuse. This cuts the power so that there is no risk of coming in contact with any live wires. Even so, it's essential to use an electrical tester that can safely determine whether any power is running through the wires you're about to work on. This device costs about $10, and lights up when power is detected. If you ask me, it's the best life insurance available. Finally, never work on electrical wires alone. If something happens, you'll want someone around to knock you away from any live wires.

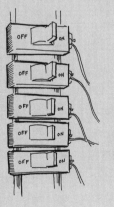

Scared? I hope so. And if this changes your mind and convinces you to hire an electrician to do any electrical work, then I've done my job.

much greater; this will likely require a carpenter to minimize the damage.

Whether you're working with a wall made of plaster or drywall, it's important to keep the speaker wire from being pinched by screws, nails, or anything else that may be hidden back there. Even a slight nick in the wiring will seriously reduce the sound quality. Also, make sure that you give yourself plenty of extra wiring to work with, both at the point where the speakers will be connected and where the wires will be attached to the receiver. If you cut the wiring too short you may not have enough to make all the connections, which would force you back to the beginning, since you cannot graft on an additional piece of wire. As a rule, leave three extra feet of wiring beyond what you think you'll need on both ends. That way you can be sure you'll have enough. It might cost a total of $1.50 in wasted wiring, but this is worth it to ensure that you haven't made an error that will make you start over. Even after you make the connection, don't be too quick to cut the excess wire. Instead, push it back slack into the wall, where it can stay in case you ever need it.

The best part about home theater setups is the prices.

I can remember building homes as recently as a few years ago, where the audio consultant would come in and I would be writing checks for $10,000 to pay them for designing and building sound systems. At last, the prices have gotten much better. I've seen systems by Sony, which is arguably one of the better names in electrical components, that sell for under $300. What does this buy you that $10,000 used to? It gets you a whole home theater system in terms of speakers and a receiver that you can plug into

Hold the TV Cabinet!

TV cabinets have become fixtures in living rooms and family rooms across the country, but they're soon likely to become a thing of the past. Plasma TVs will dominate the market within a few years. Since they're only about 3 inches thick—no matter what size the screen—they hang on the wall, with no cabinet necessary.

Tools of the Trade

Because of the risks involved, electricians insist on using rubber-handled tools for the work they do. In addition, the shafts of the screwdrivers they use tend to be several inches longer than other screwdrivers, in order to keep them a little farther away from potentially dangerous situations. If you're going to work on wiring yourself, why wouldn't you choose the same equipment that safety-conscious electricians use?

your existing television set. This will surround the room with high-quality sound, right down to those big, sub-woofer thumps and roars.

Picture, Picture

As far as the television screen goes, I have one word of advice: Less is more. Everyone seems to be spending money on large-screen TVs, in part because the prices have fallen so dramatically in recent years. TVs that have a 50-inch screen or larger, measured on the diagonal, can now be purchased for $1,000, where they used to be $6,000 and $7,000. But the thing to remember is you cannot be very close to these television sets to see the picture in the best quality. Sit closer than a dozen feet, and it will be like looking at a Seurat painting through a magnifying glass—nothing but big dots, and a fuzzy overall impression. Instead, you have to sit farther back. For instance, for a television set that has a 40-inch or 50-inch screen, the optimum viewing distance is 12 feet away. In most cases, that would be out into the next room. Unless you have a giant cavern of a room, you would be wasting your money to get a big-screen TV.

Another thing to consider is the angle at which you're watching the TV. Most TVs have to be viewed straight on to get a clear image; the angle cannot vary more than about 15 degrees off from the center. Better are the flat-screen TVs, which allow you to have a clear glimpse of the screen at an angle twice that, about 30 degrees off from the center. These allow you much more freedom in placing chairs in a living room, or wherever you have the television set up. An even better advance are the plasma TVs, which allow you clear viewing from just about any angle. These still cost thousand of dollars, but if the trends of the past are any guide to the future, the day will soon come when these will be a useful addition to any home theater. By 2010, they are expected to be the norm.

A Dim (yet Bright) Idea

Dimmer switches rank as one of the most inexpensive electrical amenities you can add to enhance your home. These allow you to control the lighting in a particular room, based on the mood you want to create. They can either be full blast for general lighting for intensive activities such as cooking and cleaning, or toned down to a gentle glow for more relaxing moments.

In general, I pay a great deal of attention to the design of dimmer switches, since some of them are easier to use than others. One of my pet peeves, in fact, is a house filled with dimmer switches that look and feel different from the rest of the switches in the house. These include the tradi-

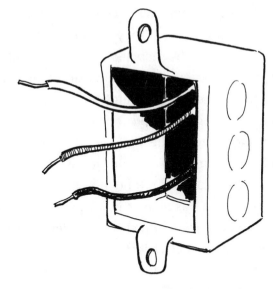

tional rheostat or rotary dimmer, which is the one that looks like a round cabinet knob, as well as the dimmer lever, which slides up. The better choice is something called a preset dimmer. This looks like a standard light switch, except that along the side it has a tiny slider that you control with your fingertip to adjust the light level. When you flick the light on, it automatically turns on to the same level at which it was last set. Dimmer switches vary in price, from about $9 to $15 apiece, not including the cost of installation. These rank as one of the great bargains in the world of home improvement.

As you choose dimmers, keep in mind that they are rated according to their wattage. Mention a word like "wattage" and most people with no electrical background instantly tune out, but this is a simple concept to understand. Most dimmers have a capacity of 600 watts, which means that you can control a maximum of six 100-watt lightbulbs with a single dimmer, or a dozen 50-watt lightbulbs, or any combination that adds up to 600 watts. Try to run an entire household off a single dimmer switch, and you're asking for trouble. The switch will overheat and burn out, which will throw the circuit breaker in an instant. Instead, depending on how many lights you're trying to control, you may have to upgrade to a larger capacity dimmer switch, designed to handle 1,000 watts or even 1,500 watts. Keep in mind that dimmer switches get warm and even hot to the touch when in use. Many times people mistakenly think this is a sign that they're overheating, but it is a perfectly normal indication that they're doing their job.

To anyone with any electrical savvy at all, installing a dimmer switch is comparatively easy. They install exactly the same way an ordinary light switch would be installed. If you don't have any electrical experience, spare yourself a ton of trouble and hire an electrician, because there are simply too many problems you might encounter along the way. If you have old cloth-covered wiring in a house, for instance, the simple act of pulling it out of the wall slightly in order to make a connection to the dimmer can cause the brittle insulation to break apart. This is truly a dangerous situation, and no amount of electrical tape can repair the problem. At this point, the wiring will have to be pulled out and replaced with new wiring, which in my view is a job for a licensed electrician. Wrapping it in electrical tape is not only a cheeseball way of doing things and a sure fire hazard, it's a violation of the national electrical code.

For those who dare, a good quality dimmer will come with easy to understand directions to make sure you're hooking everything up the right way. First, turn the power to the switch off at the circuit breaker, which will

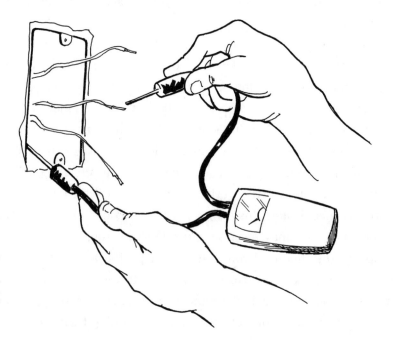

protect you while you work. Now comes the task of matching up the wires. The wires connected to both the dimmer switch and protruding from the wall are color coded, although there can be some variations in just what the colors mean, which complicates the project. The

> ## Upstairs, Downstairs
>
> Instead of hauling the central vacuum hose up and down the staircase, you can buy a separate hose for each floor. The cost for a 20-foot hose might be $150, and it will make using the central vacuum from floor to floor far easier.

white wire coming out of the back of the dimmer is the neutral wire, and should be connected to the white wire coming out of the wall. Green is always the ground wire, and should be connected to the green wire coming from the wall; the black wire is always the hot one, and should also be connected to the black wire in the wall. Now, if you look into the switch on the wall and find no white wire, no green wire, or no black wire, stop your work and head to the Yellow Pages to look under "E" for "Electrician." The risk of electrocution and creating a fire hazard by installing the switch incorrectly is too great to justify continuing with the project—especially if you don't have much experience with electricity. An electrician will be able to trace the wires back to the electrical service box to make sure exactly which one is which.

A Vacuum Cleaner Worth Bragging About

Now that you've got all these great rooms set up in your home, how are you going to keep them all clean? The best method I've found is a central vacuum.

These are actually one of the most misunderstood systems around. People imagine them to be as pricey as a Ferrari, but as with just about everything else electric, they're no longer luxuries. A top-quality vacuum can be installed for as little as $1,500, which is not much more than a high-end canister vacuum. Better yet, the central vacuum in many cases comes with a lifetime guarantee; you buy it once, and that's it. The real beauty of these devices is that you don't have to lug a vacuum cleaner around your home anymore. Instead, they contain a long hose that is inserted into various receptacles that resemble electrical outlets. The typical system by a brand such as Ametek, which is the leading manufacturer in terms of sales, has a 185-cubic-feet-per-minute capacity—two to three times that of a portable. Better yet, they have no dust-spreading exhaust system the way most conventional vacuum cleaners do.

History in a Vacuum

The idea of using in-wall plumbing to clean houses goes back to the 1850s in Sweden, where, of all things, horse-powered fans created the suction. Eventually, horses were replaced by servants who either pumped giant bellows or, in later years, pedaled stationary bicycles. Even when electric motors arrived at the turn of the twentieth century, these systems were only within reach of wealthy magnates like Henry Ford and George Eastman. Then portable vacuum cleaners hit the market in the 1920s, and their whole-house cousins were left in the dust. Central vacuums weren't forgotten entirely, though. Frank Lloyd Wright, impressed by their clutter-free convenience, specified them in a number of his later designs. The systems became more affordable in the late 1950s when plastic pipe began to replace copper, but they didn't really come into their own until the 1990s, when growing house sizes and concerns about indoor air quality coincided with improved filtration, more powerful motors, and more effective vacuum attachments.

While we see only the extended hose, the central vacuum system actually has more in common with the plumbing system. A motor, which is attached to a cylinder that looks like a midsized garbage can, mounts on the wall in the basement or first floor of the house, or sometimes even the garage. From there, plastic pipe that is about 1½ inches in diameter feeds throughout the house. It goes together just like plumbing pipes, with elbows at 90 degrees and 45 degrees for turning corners. These connect to receptacles mounted near the baseboards, which resemble large electrical outlets with a cover, that are mounted about 12 inches or so from the ground. To use the vacuum, the door on the receptacle is lifted and the hose end is inserted. An electrical connection turns the vacuum on, and the cleaning can begin. For carpets, the hose can be fitted with a beater brush, which functions just like a regular vacuum cleaner. The beauty is you'll hear nothing except suction, because the motor is in the basement or in the garage. It's a huge added-value proposition for a home, and definitely something that makes a listing sheet when a house is placed on the market for sale.

While central vacuums are easiest to install in a new house or new addition, they

A Clean Machine

One place you don't want dirt to collect is inside a central-vac motor. Before buying any system, take a close look at how easy it is to remove and clean all the filters. If you don't keep them clean, the motors will burn out sooner.

can also be retrofitted into an existing house with little trouble. Sometimes the number of receptacles have to be reduced because of the difficulty of snaking the piping in place, but this results only in the need to use a longer hose—say, 30 feet rather than 20 feet—instead of nixing the idea altogether. Whether installed into a new house or retrofitted, maintenance on the unit is minimal. You have to change and dispose of the paper filter bag every six months, and change the motor brushes every three years or so, which is a simple technique described in the instruction manual.

With these electrical gadgets wired into place, let's take a final look at what to do to make the biggest overhaul to your home—by adding an addition.

chapter SIX

The Pluses of Additions

Can't make do with the space you've got? Follow these steps to add on the rooms you need.

When assessing the way a house feels, sometimes the only way to make it work is to think beyond the walls.

This was the case with some friends named Randy and Marsha. They lived in a small Arts & Crafts bungalow that had great charm, and did most of the work on it themselves during the evenings and on weekends. They scraped woodwork to reveal the golden oak hidden beneath it, and hired someone to refinish the priceless quarter-sawn oak floors. After they had two children, however, it became clear that their home needed more than a sprucing up. It needed to become larger. "It wasn't about finding clever spaces for storage or making the most of the living room—we had literally burst at the seams," said Marsha.

There were two choices: Move, or stay put and build the extra space they needed. Here they factored their surroundings into the equation. They loved their neighborhood in suburban New Jersey, especially the tree-lined street. Since most of the houses were larger and grander than theirs, they figured any improvements they made would be more than worth it if ever they had to sell their place. "A house across the street sold for about twice what ours was worth, so we knew we could spend money safely and recoup

it if we needed to," said Randy. Working with an architect, the two created a plan that would expand the size of the house by about a third, adding a new master bedroom and bathroom upstairs, and a new kitchen and family room out the back. Despite the size of the addition, the look of the house stayed the same when viewed from the street. And when viewed from the back, the carefully done addition now looks as if it has been there all along.

With a properly conceived addition, an existing house can be completely remade. Although construction is never cheap, the savings in moving expenses and real estate commissions can help buffer the final costs. We tend to fall in love with where we're living not just because of the house, but because of our friends and neighbors nearby. Building an addition can give you the best of both worlds—a new house, in a familiar neighborhood. Moving ahead with an addition raises a range of issues that have to be addressed before the carpenters arrive, however. In the rush to get the job done, too often people end up with eyesores tacked on to the back of an otherwise beautiful house. Avoiding this pit-

Time and Materials vs. Fixed Price

In negotiating with a contractor on a cost for an addition, you have two choices. The first is a fixed price, in which the contractor quotes a price up front, and charges you only for any changes you might make throughout the process. While there is some reassurance for the homeowner in having a guaranteed price, you tend to pay more for the project since the contractor will add a buffer to protect against cost overruns. A fairer and potentially cost-saving method of billing is called "time and materials" or T & M. In this, you're charged each week for the actual time and materials involved in the project.

The key to making this system work is to manage a weekly accounting system for all charges. The contractor should present you with an itemized breakdown of the work done, including the hours workers were there, as well as receipts for materials purchased. Just because you won't know in advance the exact amount you're going to pay doesn't mean you can't get estimates of what the work will cost. The contractor should be able to give you a clear idea of the cost at the start of the project, then make adjustments along the way.

Cost overruns are inevitable. In my own house, for instance, the painter ended up charging 60 percent more than he first estimated—but that's because the job turned out to be so much more complicated than he first anticipated. If you suddenly are presented with a weekly bill that's greater than what you expected, ask politely for a justification. If the explanation suits you, fine. If not, and you continue to face higher or inexplicable charges each week that threaten to derail your budget, be willing to call the project off in mid-course and find a new contractor to complete the job.

fall requires care in terms of design and choosing the right construction materials. Architects and contractors can help create blueprints that will lead to thoughtful additions.

Let's work through the steps of an addition, which in its scope is identical to building a small house.

Bigger and Better

As homeowners inevitably discover, an addition involves a full range of construction decisions, including choices about foundations, framing, insulation, and exterior siding and masonry. For many small renovation projects, a homeowner and a contractor can sort out the details as they proceed. An addition requires more detailed advance planning, however, since it affects both the interior and exterior of the home and involves building permits. The best additions are the ones that look as if they have been there all along. And that's not something that happens by accident. It happens by design.

The first place to start is with someone who can come up with a plan that expresses in lines and material lists what you, as the homeowner, can only express in hopes and desires. The easiest way to do this is to turn to a contractor who specializes in "design-build," which means that they have the staff that can both design a project and the work crew to build it. This is a relatively new phenomenon in the last decade, and is a great way to keep the project local, since it's a little like one-stop shopping. Just as you go to Target to pick up just about everything you might need around the house, you can go to a design-build contractor to have the entire addition finished.

If you're looking for great originality and creativity, however, you'll

The Architect Litmus Test

How do you choose an architect for an addition? Personality matters, as does an architect's portfolio. Rather than looking at a scrapbook, however, ask to see some of their previous additions in person, preferably ones that have already had a chance to mature for a year or two. If you find yourself driving right by the house—because the addition blends in so well to the home and the surrounding neighborhood that you can't really distinguish it as an addition—you've found your candidate.

Surviving an Addition

In the best of circumstances, an addition can be built with a minimum disruption to the workings of a household. If you're adding an ell, or building a second floor, it's sometimes possible to isolate the work until the very last week or two. But anything else is going to resemble a whole-house renovation. You might be better off renting a house and moving out while the workers are there.

Depending on the complexity of an addition, an entire house can end up being absorbed into the construction process, and homeowners should be prepared for unexpected consequences. In an old house, the demolition of some sections can reveal rotted timbers or termite infestation that no one expected, adding both money and time to the project.

Suddenly, a small addition that was supposed to take four weeks can turn into a major makeover that lasts month, after month, after month. To be on the safe side, it's as important to think through the details of how life is going to function within a household, as it is to think about the details going into the new addition. If the kitchen is going to be demolished, for instance, take the time to have a contractor set up a temporary kitchen in the basement or another room that can actually function. Some people thrive on the inconvenience of a construction project, but for others, the stress of cooking with a hot plate and a microwave oven for two or three months is overwhelming.

Before you begin, ask yourself whether this sort of chaos is something you can handle. If it's not, then have your contractor help you figure out some alternatives.

most likely be in the market for an architect. This is someone who will help you to create a unique design for your addition, and one that you are sure won't be popping up on the neighbor's house across the street. Architects tend to be able to think with more style, and with fewer preconceived notions of what a project can be than the average design-build firm. All of this creativity comes at a cost, however. Architects typically charge a number of ways. Some will charge a flat fee, all based on time; others will charge an hourly rate, which can range from $50 to 100. In addition, some will offer services where they'll actually help you manage the construction as well, which is a percentage of the total job. If you undertake a $100,000 addition, they might charge an additional 7 to 10 percent of the total cost—including any overruns—to do the drawings and manage the project. This fee is more than worth it, especially if you're not going to be around during the days to supervise the construction. The architect can act as a "shadow-contractor," to make sure the project is proceeding as it should.

With designers and architects, you will quickly find yourself immersed not in blueprints but in something called working drawings. These are literally sketches, in various degrees of rusticity, that show the person's plans for your home. Architects or designers will literally come into your home, often sitting with you around the kitchen table, and start working on drawings that they hope will capture what it is you need in terms of an addition. The drawings are designed for you to spend time with, to mull over, to disagree with, and to eventually focus on a direction for a plan. They're far cheaper than actual blueprints, because they're nothing but sketches. It's also far easier to change things on paper than it is when the addition is framed with 2 by 4s and covered with drywall.

In general, I have found, people do not spend enough time with working drawings. Maybe they think the sketches aren't real, or maybe they think they'll have a better idea of what the project will look like once it's up. Most likely, they fail to realize that this

A Matter of Time

In planning for an addition, make sure you leave plenty of time for the approval process of your plans, especially if any zoning changes or variances will be needed. To be on the safe side, double the time estimate. If you think it will take three months, plan for six instead.

is the moment where the design occurs; changes farther down the line are going to be more expensive and more difficult to make. I would recommend taking these drawings and taping them to the hallway, or to the wall where the addition is planned, and living with them for at least a week. Invite friends and family over, have a party, and solicit everyone's opinions about what works, and what doesn't. I've done several projects where the owners have not ultimately been happy with what we've done—because they didn't spend enough time to think things through.

Once the finished drawings are completed, they then go to your local city or town building department for approvals and permits. This is a larger hurdle than it might seem, even with an architect involved. The reason is that many local building inspectors enforce various aspects of the building codes differently.

Just know that even having all the finished drawings and all the permits in place doesn't mean the process is over. As you're building your addition, you will inevitably discover small things that you wish had been different. Maybe the opening to a room is too narrow, or in the wrong place, and you don't notice this until the framing process and even the wiring and the drywall is in place. Should you keep quiet about it? No. Don't worry about making the changes at this state. It's much cheaper to change a couple of 2 by 4s during the framing stage than it is to change cabinets or flooring or fireplace mantels or built-in bookcases at a later date. Unless you build houses every day, a construction site is a muddle until the drywall goes up. At that point, make whatever changes you want. Moving a doorway or adding a window might cost a few hundred dollars more, but this is a one-time expense, compared to the cost of living with your mistake every day you own your home.

Looking Good

We all want our homes to look good, but when building an addition it's especially important for it to look good from the outside. This is where many people run into a ditch. They get so focused on their specific needs inside—whether it's an extra bedroom for the kids, or a big family room out the back—that they lose all sense of what the thing will look like. Suddenly, a giant projection like a rocket launch tower will rise from the roof of an otherwise charming Cape, or a rectangular wing will jut like a bowling alley off the back of a quaint farmhouse. As Frank Lloyd Wright once said, "Proportion is to architecture what location is to real estate. In short, it's everything." This is an important thing to remember for anyone building an addition. So many times I see gigantic additions that dwarf the original house, like Goliath sitting on top of David's head. If you're taking this route, you'll do much better by reinventing the entire façade and calling it a new house, rather than trying to make it blend in to the forlorn little remnants of the original.

The very character of a home is at risk when considering an addition.

A Georgian brick revival, for instance, can be ruined with the inappro-priate addition of a white clapboard ell in the back. A bland tract home from the '60s, on the other hand, can be reborn with a well thought-out addition that gives it new lines and a new style. Proportion is an art, not a science. You can't just select a set of windows, a type of roof, a few doors, put them together, and call it an addition. You might end up with a dream house, but then again, you might end up with a Frankenstein house. Since there's no formula for good aesthetics, it's best to get some serious help. Find the best architect or contractor-designer you can, and go slowly. If you rush through the planning stages of an addition, you will likely end up making a regrettable mistake.

When planning an addition, it can be hard to imagine what the over-all impact of it will be on the existing house. You want to be confident about what you're building. And the more you can visualize it, the bet-ter off you'll be. This used to be done with models and drawings. One excellent alternative today, however, is with virtual design software. These are professional software programs that, in the hands of an expe-

rienced designer or architect, can produce astonishingly realistic rendi-
tions of your proposed addition. Some involve taking digital photo-
graphs of the house and grafting the proposed expansion onto the
image. The result, when printed out, looks exactly like a snapshot of the
house with all the additions in place. It's like seeing a picture of the house
already finished, which makes it easy to form an opinion about whether
you like it or not.

The most sophisticated software programs also make it possible to
create a three-dimensional view of the interior and exterior of the addi-

Walls Without the Commitment

While virtual reality software programs can help people visualize the interior of an addition, I also like a hammer-and-nails approach. Before adding partition walls in an addition, I sometimes build temporary walls framed with 2 by 4s to give homeowners a feel for the size of the rooms—before the layout becomes permanent. It's one thing to see the size of a room on a blueprint; it's another to actually stand in it and be able to say with certainty that it is exactly what you want.

tion, with all of its décor and landscaping in place. Besides giving the homeowners a preview of what they will get, it also helps the architect identify design flaws that might otherwise be hard to spot. When an architect is drawing by hand, it's often possible to make mistakes such as sketching a roof that in reality won't align, or a doorway that has an opening too high to line up with the tops of the windows. And you might not find any of this out until you reach the construction site. Those mistakes are impossible to make with virtual programs, however; what you see is what you get.

One caveat: These are professional tools, best used in the hands of professionals. Just because you can go to an office supply store and fish a software design program out of the $9.99 bin doesn't mean you'll get anywhere near the same results, any more than getting hold of a paintbrush will automatically turn you into Picasso.

Adding Up

Now that we've reviewed the process of designing an addition, let's go into greater detail about what the possibilities are. In expanding a home, there are two basic possibilities. You can add out into the yard, or you can add up into an additional story. Let's begin with the high-rise approach to additions. In most cases, going up is more cost effective,

Planning a Schedule

Although there can be no standard schedule for how long building an addition will take, there can be a rough timeline for the steps involved before an addition can even begin. Here are some major steps, working backward from the desired start date:

12 to 18 months before the start date:

Begin researching what you'd like by looking at magazines, other homes, and showrooms. Start creating an idea file as well as a wish list, making two separate columns for things you need, and things you would like.

10 to 12 months:

Begin figuring out a budget for the addition, and checking about a bank loan. Also, begin asking family and friends to recommend architects, designers, and contractors.

6 to 8 months:

Interview architects, contractors, and designers. Bring them your idea file and wish list.

4 to 6 months:

Refine the plan down to a detailed spec sheet. If a roof is specified as shingle roof, that's not enough. It should say, "25-year-fiberglass shingles, 3-tab, at $35 a square." Also, now is the time to file for any required variances from planning, zoning, or historic commissions.

2 to 4 months:

Solicit competitive bids or negotiate with one selected contractor, if you have a preference. After choosing the contractor, decide on start and finish dates, then have an attorney review the contract before signing it.

1 month:

Make sure the contractor secures building permits. Now is the time to make any final selections, such as appliances, cabinets, and windows.

Foundation Support

If a foundation is deemed unable to support an additional story, it can be buttressed through a technique called a helical pier system. Supporting posts are literally corkscrewed into the ground under high pressure, and pinned to the footings at the base of the foundation wall. Most municipalities around the country permit this as an acceptable way to buttress an existing foundation, which spares homeowners the enormous expense of jacking up the house in order to pour a new one.

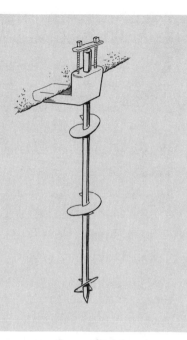

and, as a result, is by far the most common addition. It does not involve adding a foundation, and the existing mechanical systems such as the plumbing and wiring are already in place. In some communities, the size of the footprint—or floor plan—of a house is tightly regulated through zoning, which means the only opportunity for expansion may be to go up.

Common as it is, adding or expanding a second story involves some careful considerations, mostly to insure that the structure of the existing house is adequate enough to support the additional weight of the second story. While adding a new floor can be an economical way to increase the size of a house, such additions can be extremely weighty and easily top 100 tons, give or take a few grand pianos. You can't just start building and hope it all holds together. Instead, the house has to have a careful inspection of the foundation and the existing beams to determine whether they're strong enough to hold the weight of the new addition. This is where a structural engineer or an architect can come in handiest. In a one-story house, it is all but guaranteed that the existing ceiling

Managing the Building Inspector

I have a concept for a screenplay that I think could make a movie studio a lot of money. At the very least, movie theaters from coast to coast would be packed with contractors. The movie would be called *The Attack of the 50-Foot Building Inspector,* and it would involve the hilarious exploits of a building inspector on a rampage—making homeowners rip out insulation they had just installed because it wasn't done perfectly, forcing them to have an architect redraw expensive blueprints because they weren't done on the right paper, and making an entire construction crew wait for days until he manages to mosey on over to approve the electrician's wiring.

Building inspectors serve vital tasks, of course. These local agents make sure that anything built in their community is done so according to current building codes and other standards. This results in better, safer homes for all. It also results in a lot of gray hair for anyone trying to manage the process. The reason is that the relationship with a building inspector often deteriorates into a clash of personalities. Homeowners are trying to move the project along so that they don't have to pay for needless delays, contractors want to build the project according to the way they think will be best, and building inspectors often have their own

structure will not be strong enough to support an additional story. Instead, a new floor plate, as it is called, will have to be added. The foundation, too, also deserves the sort of inspection that only a trained engineer can perform.

One of the first things the engineer will examine is the main beam spanning the length of the basement ceiling. If it's too weak, it can be strengthened with support columns or by adding additional beams—a process called sistering—alongside it. A foundation wall rests on a wide concrete base called a footing, which helps stabilize the entire structure by distributing the sheer load of a home over a greater surface area. Foundations with footings that measure 2 feet wide by 1 foot deep should set of details that have particular importance to them.

If you're working on a small project, there's no choice but to give the building inspectors what they want. For a larger project, however, I would advocate hiring a person known as a "permitting expediter." This could be the architect, the contractor, or someone who works for either of them. The point is to pay someone who already knows the building inspector from previous projects to shepherd your plans through the approval process. It might cost you $500 to hire someone to do this, but it can save you far more in aggravation and delays, especially when the project involves a major addition.

easily support a second story. But smaller footings, which an engineer can identify, could spell trouble. A footing's size would be difficult and costly to change. But most foundations I've seen, even old brick and stone ones, could probably carry the weight of another story with little trouble. Still, this is not something you want to guess at; get a structural engineer involved.

Adding Out

Not every house can or should be added onto. If you've got a two-story home on a suburban street, for instance, the chances are slim that local zoning codes will allow you to add a third story. In these cases, adding out may make the best option. This is the costlier route, however, because it involves enlarging the footprint of a house and building a new foundation. In addition, it will almost certainly trigger a tax increase, since it will raise the actual square footage of a home on which most assessments are based. Let's take a closer look at some of the issues involved.

Even the smallest addition—a simple set of brick or stone steps, for instance, or a screened-in porch—requires a solid foundation. Without it, the new structure would soon settle and twist away from the original house. There are no shortcuts when it comes to a foundation. It's a "do it right, or don't do it at all" proposition. What type of foundation is needed depends on what part of the country an addition is being built in. In cold-winter areas, a full foundation that extends from between 4 to 8 feet into the ground would inevitably be required. This gives the base of the foundation, called the footings, a solid hold in ground that does not freeze, no matter how cold it gets. That way, you can be sure the foundation won't heave and ruin the addition as the seasons change. In frost-free parts of the country, there's additional latitude with foundation construction. Shallower walls are possible, and in some cases additions can even be built on concrete slabs that are poured onto, rather than in, the ground.

House foundations are notoriously vulnerable to infiltration by water. Basements can flood, but even crawl spaces can be damaged by prolonged dampness. In addition, moisture leads to mildew, and creates a hospitable environment for wood-devouring insects. The number one enemy of a house is water. And the foundation is where the battle against it begins.

To keep ground moisture and runoff from making their way through a new foundation, the walls have to be waterproofed. In the past, this has involved covering them with a thick, tarry asphalt. The problem with this is that as the foundation settles over time, it inevitably becomes filled with small cracks the asphalt does not seal. This results in leaks. A better

Garage, Sweet Home

In a house pinched for space, nothing seems more inviting than an attached garage. There it is, an extra 400 or 500 square feet already built and attached to the house, and just waiting for colonization. Turning a garage into living space can work well in some cases, as long as you adhere to a few basic design principles.

The first involves some simple logistics about the foundation. Garages tend to be lower than the rest of the house, and have a floor made from a cold, concrete slab. You can't just throw tiles or carpeting over this and expect it to be comfortable, especially in the winter when you're trying to heat the space. Instead, a new floor needs to be framed over this. This solves a couple of problems at once. It gives you a chance to insulate beneath it, and it also gives you a chance to raise the height of the floor so it matches the floors in the existing house. One warning: Concrete tends to expand and contract with the seasons. If you attach the new floor to the concrete, it, too, will heave and could create havoc. Instead, the floor should be framed in such a way that it spans the concrete beneath it, without actually touching it.

Now that it's evolving into living space, the exterior of the garage needs some special attention. The garage doors will disappear, leaving a blank slate of possibilities. This is a great opportunity to add bay or bow windows to tie the new room into the rest of the house. While you're at it, take a close look at the entryway between the new room and the existing mudroom or kitchen that connects to the main portion of the house. Where possible, widen this to create a hallway, rather than keep it as a narrow doorway. This will help mask the fact that the doorway once led out to the cars.

Since the foundation, framing, roofing, and most of the siding is already in place, you can expect to save at least half the cost of a brand-new addition of a similar size.

What's in a Foundation?

The crucial component of any foundation wall lies at its base. There it widens into poured-concrete blocks called footings. The foundation walls transfer the load of the house directly to the footings. Footings, in turn, distribute this weight over a broader area of undisturbed soil than the walls alone would, and thus prevent settling or movement of the structure above. Typically a footing is poured 4 to 8 inches thick, and twice as wide as the wall sitting on top of it. An 8-inch wall, for example, would require a 16-inch footing.

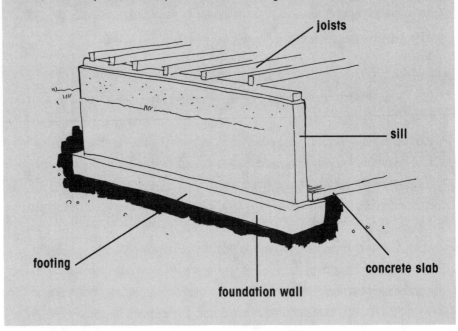

approach to waterproofing can be found in a giant rubberized membrane that is literally wrapped around the exterior wall of the foundation and mechanically fastened in place. This membrane operates on the same principle as a "run-flat" tire on a car: If it is penetrated, the membrane seals itself back up, which reduces the potential of a water leak. Protection of this sort does cost extra. While it might cost $1,000 to have ordinary asphalt sprayed onto a foundation, the rubberized membrane could cost $2,500 or even more. The extra money is worth it, however, in order to assure a dry basement.

An additional measure of protection can be gained by adding something known as interior drain tile. This amounts to adding a piping system around the perimeter of the basement down by the footings, and is pitched so that it drains into a pit sunken into the basement floor. Even if you have properly waterproofed walls, water can still seep beneath the footings, and that's what this system is designed to eliminate. Where dampness is a problem, a sump pump can be installed in the pit, that collects the water and evacuates it out into the yard or into a sewer system. It's expensive to add an interior drain system such as this after a foundation is built; in all cases, it makes better sense to install it beforehand as a precaution to protect against flooding.

An Outside Job

An addition can remake a home, but renovations can also be accomplished from the outside, in the form of landscaping. This helps tie a new addition into the existing house, creating an overall harmonious look.

Landscaping inevitably involves foundation plantings, which help a house look like it's nestled into its setting rather than standing starkly on top of it. Before the plantings go in, however, the area around the foundation has to be checked for proper drainage. Soil that is compacted here following construction can result in what is called a negative grade or downward slope toward the walls. That can cause damp basements. To remedy this, the soil should be reconfigured so that it has a pitch away from the house a minimum of 1 inch in elevation for every 8 feet.

With the grading corrected, you can turn to planting. One obvious problem when planting is to try to crowd too many things together. Instead, foundation plantings need at last three years to mature, along with plenty of room to fill out. Crowded plants may look luxuriant at first, but they will soon aggravate problems such as dampness, mildew, rot, and even termites, especially if they rub against wood siding. That is why landscape designers always plant at least 18 inches to 2 feet away from the house. One way to help foundation plantings seem lush as they mature is to fill in gaps with annuals or perennials. As the larger plantings grow, these smaller ones can then be removed and transplanted elsewhere.

Another essential exterior element is the drainage system, in the form of downspouts and gutters. Clogged gutters can be the cause of a wet basement, since the water then spills over the edge and tends to pool in one place near the foundation. When building an addition, this is a good time to add what are known as leafless gutters, which have a cover on them that keeps them free and clear. The one shortcoming of these gutters is that in a torrential rain they have a slightly reduced flow compared to ordinary gutters. You can expect some rain to wash off the roof and spill over the edge. This is a small problem compared to the larger advantages, however. Leafless gutters tend to be expensive; you might spend from $6 to $12 a foot compared to $2 to $3 for ordinary gutters. Is it worth the price? In my opinion, yes—especially if it prevents you from falling off a ladder during an annual gutter-cleaning ritual.

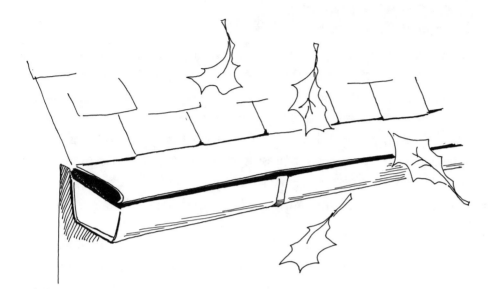

A Parting Word

As we look at the rooms in our homes in an attempt to revitalize them, we are sometimes overtaken by an urge to do everything quickly. We make a radical plan, search for a contractor who is available immediately, and rush to have everything completed. I have one word of advice in this regard: Relax. Take a slow-and-steady approach, so that you can be sure the changes you make will be done well and that they satisfy what it is you are trying to accomplish with your home.

Too often, in the zeal to have things finished, we push ahead with projects that are out of sync. We paint, before taking care of the electrical systems; we redo the floors and install carpeting, before realizing that the plumbing system needs to be overhauled; we hastily plan an addition, before realizing that by paring down some unwanted possessions and reconfiguring closets we don't really need the extra space.

In all cases, a slow-and-steady approach works best. Where possible, work on one room at a time, and finish it, from floor to ceiling. This will give you peace of mind as you approach the remaining rooms in your

Up with Downspouts

Downspouts, as their name suggests, carry water from the gutters that run along the edges of a roof down to the ground, where it is then shunted away from the house. In an attempt to make the exterior of their homes look less cluttered, many homeowners limit the number of downspouts they install, which limits the drainage potential of the gutters. To keep a dry basement, I recommend adding as many downspouts as possible, no matter what it looks like. You'll need at least one for every 15 to 20 feet of roofing.

home. In moments of despair, of which there are bound to be more than a few, you'll be able to look to that one room as inspiration, to know that you'll be able to achieve the same top-quality results wherever you focus your time and your talents.

The result will be a place that unfolds around you, in keeping with your budget and your vision of what things should be.

The result will be a house you can truly call home.

Appendix

Resources to Remember
Need more information to help transform the rooms in your home? Start the journey here.

When it comes to remaking your home, too much of anything is usually bad—except with regard to information. The more you know, the better you'll be able to sort through the options, from refinishing the floors to choosing materials for drapes. The more you know, the more you can turn this to your advantage in creating a home that suits you best. And the more you know, the more you'll be able to manage the squadron of contractors and subcontractors who will likely be doing much of the work. No list of resources will ever be complete, but I've narrowed down the possibilities to include some that I rely on that I know will help get you started. Where they exist, I've included toll-free numbers, but try the Web sites first. You'll save time, and probably find everything you need without having to wait for the mail to arrive.

American Furniture Manufacturers Association

www.afma4u.org

P.O. Box HP-7

High Point, NC 27261

336-884-5000

Click under the "Consumers Looking for Furniture" on this Web site to access detailed information about choosing furniture by style and price.

American Institute of Architects

www.aia.org

1735 New York Ave., NW

Washington, DC 20006

800-AIA-3837

Use this Web site to find books and design resources, as well as a licensed architect to help turn your kitchen dreams into a workable plan.

American Lighting Association

www.americanlightingassoc.com

P.O. Box 420288

Dallas, TX 75342

800-274-4484

Look on the Web site under "lighting tips and information" for pointers on kitchen lighting; spend $5, and get a booklet on tips for lighting the whole house.

American Society for Home Inspectors

www.ashi.com
932 Lee Street
Suite 101
Des Plaines, IL 60016
847-759-2820/800-743-ASHI

Rather than guessing what's wrong with your home, consult this Web site to find home inspectors in your area. They'll be able to tell you exactly what needs fixing, from major systems to minor ones.

American Society of Interior Designers

www.asid.org
608 Massachusetts Ave., NE
Washington, DC 20002
202-546-3480

For a list of licensed interior designers in your area start here; also includes tips on how to work with one once you've hired them.

Better Homes and Gardens Magazine

www.bhg.com
Meredith Corporation
1716 Locust Street
Des Moines, IA 50309-3023

Search this Web site to find volumes of information about how to remake a room and choose materials, from paints to draperies.

Carpet and Rug Institute

www.carpet-rug.com
P.O. Box 2048
Dalton, GA 30722
800-882-8846

Consult this Web site to find details on everything from selecting carpeting to hiring a carpet-cleaning professional.

Closet Maid

www.closetmaid.com
Emerson Storage Solutions
P.O. Box 4100
8000 West Florissant Avenue
St. Louis, MO 63136-8506
800-874-0008

This Web site, run by one of the leading closet-organization companies, can provide you with details on how to design storage spaces ranging from closets to utility rooms.

Color Marketing Group

www.colormarketing.org
5904 Richmond Hwy.
#408
Alexandria, VA 22303
703-329-8500

On this entertaining Web site, you can learn about such things as forecasting color trends and the history of color, from basic black, to today's iridescent effects.

DoItYourself.Com

www.doityourself.com

Find answers to questions on this Web site, including how to hang wallpaper, install new windows, and frame an addition, as well as how to use a home equity loan to pay for it all.

Hometime.Com

www.hometime.com

The Web site for this popular TV show is a great how-to source for household projects you can tackle yourself, along with a resource guide for books, videos, and manufacturers.

International Association of Lighting Designers

www.iald.org
Suite 9-104
The Merchandise Mart
Chicago, IL 60654
312-527-3677

Designed for the building trade, this Web site contains everything you could possibly want to know about lighting, as well as tips for working with lighting designers.

National Association of the Remodeling Industry

www.nari.org
780 Lee St.
Suite 200
Des Plaines, IL 60016
800-611-NARI (6274)/847-298-9200

A search of this Web site will yield a gallery of project ideas, such as the best additions for under $100,000 and the best whole-house makeovers.

National Fire Protection Association

www.nfpa.org
1 Batterymarch Park
Quincy, MA 02269
800-344-3555/617-770-3000

Do a search on this Web site to learn about how to use a fire extinguisher, install smoke detectors and carbon monoxide protectors, as well as to download a tip sheet on improving fire safety throughout the house.

Wallcoverings Association

www.wallcoverings.org
401 N. Michigan Avenue
Chicago, IL 60611
312-644-6610

Click on this Web site to learn the basics of wallpapering, including a do-it-yourself guide, information on styles of wallpaper, as well as wallpaper history.

Window Coverings Association of America

www.wcaa.org
3550 McKelvey Road, Suite 202C
Bridgeton, MO 63044-2535
888-298-9222

Although directed toward interior decorators, this Web site has plenty of information that can be of use to homeowners—particularly the "Windows and Coverings Forum," which includes useful tips from the pros.

About the Authors

Lou Manfredini started working in a hardware store when he was thirteen years old. He worked as a carpenter's apprentice in college and opened his own construction company in Chicago in 1985. His media career began ten years later when he pitched the idea of a call-in show to a local radio station. WGN-AM picked up the show, and Mr. Fix-It was born. The radio show is now nationally syndicated, and Lou is also a frequent contributor to television and print media, as well. He appears regularly on the *Today Show,* and has a bimonthly column in *USA Weekend.* He still runs his own construction company, and actively builds and renovates homes. Lou lives in Chicago with his wife and four children.

Curtis Rist, an award-winning journalist and author, began his home improvement career a decade ago when he attended house building school, then designed and helped construct his own house. He is a former senior writer at *This Old House* magazine and the coauthor of the *This Old House Homeowner's Manual.* Inspired by working with Lou on their first book, *House Smarts,* he began a new career as a contractor—and now buys and renovates old houses in Hudson, New York, where he lives with his wife and two sons.

Get a better fix on your home-improvement needs with Lou Manfredini's expert advice

How an intuitive understanding of your home will help you make the right decisions for its future, as well as your own

Why it's so important to set your standards high—for yourself, your contractor, and your materials

The secrets to taming those monsters of the basement: dampness, darkness, concrete floors, and low ceilings

Why the best way to keep that roof over your head is to know how to maintain it

The truth behind that most essential and trouble-prone room of the house: the bathroom

What you've always wanted to know about closets but were afraid to ask

member Mr. Fix-It's 3 rules:

ve fun.

to be smarter than the 'terials you're working with.

'...never hold a nail for someone else.

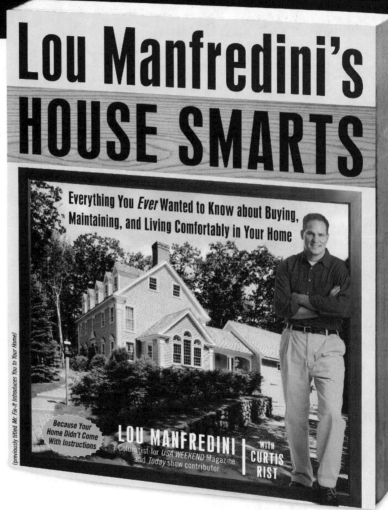

A BALLANTINE BOOKS TRADE PAPERBACK

Available wherever books are sold

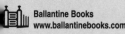

Transform a worn-out kitchen into your pride and joy

- Incorporate elements of expensive kitchens into your design

- Tackle intimidating tasks, from new floors to countertops

- Freshen up your cabinets with a dazzling "reface" lift

- Figure out the best ways to bring in natural as well as electric lighting

- Confront issues such as plumbing, color schemes, and layout

- Discover which projects require expert assistance—and which you can handle yourself

- Avoid pitfalls and ask your contractor the right questions

- Improve and add value to your home

Includes illustrations, anecdotes, specific prices, essential tips, and a lifetime of insight

Lou Manfredini's KITCHEN SMARTS

Make over your kitchen with minimum fuss

- *Save thousands of dollars with handy homebuilders' secrets*

- *Expert advice on "do it yourself" projects*

- *Learn when to get a contractor, and at the lowest cost*

LOU MANFREDINI
Columnist for *USA WEEKEND* Magazine and *Today* show contributor
WITH CURTIS RIST

A BALLANTINE BOOKS TRADE PAPERBACK
Available wherever books are sold

Ballantine Books
www.ballantinebooks.com

For more information about MR. FIX-IT, visit www.hammerandnail.com